'ALL IN A LIfeiime'

The story of a Dalesman as told to June Fisher

By June Fisher

June Fisher

Compiled by Anne Bonney

Aided by Bryan Lancaster's Trust - Friends' Gift Estate

"Settle Monthly Meeting of the Religious Society of Friends welcomes and supports the publication of this autobiography of our Member, James Fisher"

Dedicated to my grandchildren
Mark, Jayne and Simon

Published by Helm Press
10 Abbey Gardens, Natland, Kendal, Cumbria LA9 7SP
Tel: 015395 61321

First published 1999

Typeset in Bitstream Baskerville 8, 9 & 11pt

ISBN 0 9531836 3 7

Typeset and printed by Miller Turner Printers Ltd
The Sidings, Beezon Fields, Kendal, Cumbria, LA9 6BL Tel: 01539 740937

Cover: Town End, Bentham about 1910 with a dustcart on the right.
By kind permission of Bernard Williams

CONTENTS

INTRODUCTION

It was in the summer of 1993, after mother, Mary Fisher's death in March that dad, James Fisher, or Jim, as he likes to be known, decided to apply for a room at Abbeyfield House, Main Street, High Bentham. He was successful and John, his son and myself, his daughter-in-law, helped him choose suitable furniture and moved him to his new home. The remaining household items were duly dispersed and the house put up for sale.

It was whilst we were clearing the garage that we came across an old tin trunk which on opening appeared to be full of snow. It was very dry and powdery. On closer examination we discovered old books and a photograph album. Some of the photographs had become loose and were lying in the bottom of the trunk and appeared to be rather damp. All the contents were covered with the snowy substance and nothing on the photographs was discernible. I put the whole lot into a dustbin bag and took them home.

The following morning heralded a warm, sunny day, so tying a scarf around my nose and mouth, I laid the photographs outside in the sunshine and as they dried, I cleaned them carefully with a soft brush. You can imagine my delight when from beneath all the mildew appeared beautiful sepia photographs. There was no one John or I recognised and I couldn't wait to take them over to Bentham to find out who they were.

As dad identified photograph after photograph I became very interested in his past, something he hardly ever talked about. He was still very much in mourning for Mary and finding coming to terms with her death very difficult. Nevertheless, on my frequent visits to Abbeyfield House, little anecdotes about his early years began to unfold.

I felt now that it wouldn't be too upsetting for him if we delved further into his life story. It was one Wednesday morning in February 1998, that I arrived at his room armed with an A4 notebook and pen. When I suggested that we should write down what he could remember of his life, he was delighted. We started as far back as he could remember, which was back in 1906-7. As the story grew, I was astounded by his marvellous memory.

Written by me, in his own words, you can read his recollections for yourself. It is written down as accurately as Jim can remember so please excuse any slight errors along the way.

Special thanks go to everyone who contributed photographs and helped in anyway towards the successful completion of this book. I am particularly grateful for the help given by David Johnson, Bernard Williams, Mary Butterfield and Jim's niece, Robin Oliver. My thanks to the Settle Society of Friends for their encouragement and the Bryan Lancaster's Trust - Friends' Gift Estate (A Quaker Trust) for their kind gift towards publication.

Please read on and enjoy 'All in a Lifetime'.

June Fisher

Spring 1999

Jim taken in his room at Abbeyfield House, High Bentham, in 1998

"I am ninety-five years old now and this is an
account of my life as I remember it".

5

My father James Fisher and my mother Edith (nee Crummock) on their wedding day in 1900

Chapter One
MY EARLY YEARS IN BURTON-IN-LONSDALE

I am ninety-five years old now and this is an account of my life as I remember it. My father, James Fisher, was one of three children, all born in a house in the High Street, Burton-in-Lonsdale and my mother Edith (nee Crummock), was one of three children from Leeds.

During the late 1800's and early 1900's, a vicar from Leeds brought a group of children from his church, annually to Burton-in-Lonsdale, to camp in the showfield which led off from the corner of Low Street and Duke Street. Edith Crummock was a young girl helper and was very pretty with a mass of beautiful hair. She worked for Burton's Tailors in Leeds. It was during one of these visits that my father met her in 1898 and courting commenced.

In the year 1900, my father James and Edith were married in Leeds. It was a big wedding and the reception was held in one of the rooms in the Town Hall. They went to live in Liverpool where they managed a public house near to the waterfront. The inn was in Scotland Road, off the Bootle Docks. An overhead railway ran around the docks and stretched five and a half miles between Dingle and Seaforth Sands. I believe it was also quite a tourist attraction in those days being used by people going to work or viewing the great liners. Scotland Road was rather a dangerous place to live, so I was told, mostly due to foreign shipping bringing in hordes of thirsty, rowdy sailors. They drank too much, became quarrelsome and nearly always ended up fighting. My father owned a pistol which he carried with him at all times. It was never used but was there for protection. My parents owned other properties in Liverpool, so were comfortably off.

My sister Agnes was born on 29th July 1902 and I, James born on 22nd June 1904, at 118 Ruskin Street, Liverpool. During the early part of their marriage, my cousin Edgar stayed with them and every day they took him to the hospital in Liverpool for treatment on his twisted foot. The twist was completely cured after about a year. Early in 1906, my parents sold up in Liverpool and temporarily lived up Springfield, in High Bentham. My father went into partnership with John Fisher, his brother. They had a drapery business but soon afterwards my parents decided to go into business on their own and bought a quaint country inn called the 'Hen and Chickens'. It was built in an almost Tudor style and dated in the early 17th century. There were mullioned windows with leaded lights and a large creaking sign hung over into the High Street of the small West Yorkshire village called Burton-in-Lonsdale.

There were several potteries in the village, one on the corner of the High Street, almost opposite the 'Hen and Chickens' and when the kilns were packed, stoked and fired a thick haze rested over the village, thus giving it the nickname, 'Black Burton'. It was a cruel name for such a picturesque spot. Altogether over the years there were thirteen potteries in the village.

Small industries flourished at that time and there were three or four public

Low Street, Burton-in-Lonsdale in 1911. The spire of All Saints Church is in the distance

8

houses, I believe ten at one time. As I remember there were four small shops. Tatham's shop was in Duke Street and sold everything from paraffin to cheese. It had a stone flagged floor and a strong smell of lamp oil. When the shop door bell jangled, a very small, elderly Mrs Tatham appeared behind the long wooden counter. She always wore black and had a black velvet band round her throat, with some kind of cameo brooch attached to the front of it.

Annie Harrison had a sweet shop at the bottom of Duke Street, facing down Low Street. She always wore a mop cap and pumps, with holes cut in the sides to accommodate her bunions. She sold other things besides sweets but her shop always smelled pleasantly of aniseed. The other shop as I remember, was a grocer's shop on the High Street, but I can't recall the owner's name. A small baker's shop two doors up from the 'Hen and Chickens' was owned by the Brayshaw family. There was a Post Office at the east end of the High Street, run by a man and his two unmarried daughters. They were called Maxfield.

The Tatham family had a coal business next to their shop in Duke Street. They also had a horse and trap taxi service, which was mostly used to transport people to and from the railway stations at Ingleton and Bentham. There was a blacksmith's shop nearby, owned by the Slater family and several joiner's shops. When the weather cock was recently brought down from the church spire for gilding, the name 'Slater' was stamped along the lower edge.

I remember at a very early age, perhaps three years old, going with my sister Agnes, down to Annie Harrison's to spend our halfpenny, (a week's pocket money) on sweets. We always bought mint imperials but I never managed to get mine home. There were many youngsters in the village in the early 1900's and plenty of friends to share them with (cupboard love!)

My sister and I attended the village school, the Richard Thornton Endowed School. I started at the tender age of three. Two of the teachers at that time were Mr Mayall and Miss Nanny Bateson. I always carried a small stick with me. I suppose it became my trade mark and is evident on early photographs.

One day I dared to climb the sweet chestnut tree in the school playground (it is still there). Unfortunately, I fell and still bear the scar over my eyebrow to this day, ninety-two years later. My early days at school were happy days and both Agnes and I enjoyed them.

We usually set off early to school, me in my short trousers, knee socks and hob nail shoes and Agnes in dresses and pinafores often made by mother. We always played the game of marbles on the way to school. The marbles were pot and mostly taken out of the tops of pop and beer bottles. We etched a ring in the earth and put our marbles inside. Each player had a large marble with which he, or she, would aim, or fire at the smaller ones in the ring. Any we knocked out of the ring, we kept. There was never time to play on the way home to lunch, which consisted of a snack meal of sandwiches, or jam and bread, which I always enjoyed. In cold weather mother often made soup for us.

Other games we enjoyed were whip and top and trundling a hoop. I remember owning a splendid iron hoop, with a metal hook to control it. Ball games were also

Richard Thornton Endowed School, Burton-in-Lonsdale, around 1908

Burton-in-Lonsdale Sunday School about 1909

First row, left to right, third boy from end is Jim Fisher. Second back row, fourth person in is Agnes Fisher with bow in her hair.

Robin Oliver, Australia

enjoyed and pigs bladders were often inflated and used as footballs or handballs.

We played tick and tack (I think that is what it was called), with a flat piece of wood hollowed out at one end to hold a small wooden ball. The wood was then hit with a stout stick and when the ball flipped into the air, we had to try to hit it.

Skipping was a very healthy exercise which we greatly enjoyed either individually or in threes, two twirling the rope and one skipping in and out.

Singing games were quite popular but I don't recall any of the words, although I always enjoyed singing.

A small girl of my own age, called Molly Bateson and myself had sweet singing voices and often sang together standing on stools in front of the class. I remember making a very early recording with Molly at Greeta House. We sang 'The Dear Little Shamrock of Ireland' and we were recorded by Mr Horner, who was one of the first people to have recording equipment.

I don't remember too much about those early years at school, except perhaps, some of my friends, my best one being, Tom Blacow. Others were Dora Tatham, Harriet Slater, The Waggett brothers, Richard Edmondson, Peter Bateson, Marie Horner, John James Edmondson, Maggie Coats, Alice (Topper) Harrison, Bessie Harrison and Johnny Nelson. (Alice earned the nickname 'Topper' for being extremely pretty and was known by this name all her life).

My parents went to church on Sundays. Children were not really encouraged to attend services in those days. The adult members of the congregation seemed to like the peace and quiet for meditation.

There were two services, morning at 10.30 am and evening at 6.30 pm and the six church bells were rung before each. After church, we all sat down to a wonderful Sunday lunch, cooked by mother. I don't remember whether father grew anything in our long garden but we always had plenty of fresh fruit and vegetables. Lunch having been eaten, Agnes and I went along to the well attended Sunday School with our many friends. It was held in the building originally called the Sunday School and which is now the village hall in the High Street.

Mother was a good cook and always made her own bread, only occasionally buying from Brayshaws' Bakery next door. There were oil lamps in all the downstairs rooms and we had candles to see us to bed but we always blew them out before we settled to sleep. It surprises me that there weren't more house fires with so many open flames around!

There was a wash house at the back where mother did the weekly wash which was pegged out to dry down the long, back garden which faced south, making a good drying ground. Later saw mother busily ironing with her flat irons in the kitchen where they were heated on a big, black kitchen range. She had several of these irons, all of different sizes.

I had relatives at Burton-in-Lonsdale, who lived in the village and farmed at Gallaber. They were my Uncle Tom, father's brother, his wife, Mary and my four cousins, Agnes, Arthur, Edgar and Norman. Aunt Mary, for some reason always called me Jammie and used to catch me on my way home from school to run errands for her. Another uncle, Harry Fearn and his wife, Jane, lived on the High Street and had two children, Annie and Tom. Harry Fisher, one of my father's older brothers lived in Arkholme. He taught at the school in Hornby and sadly collapsed on the boat returning from a holiday in the Isle of Man and died shortly afterwards.

Uncle Herbert, Aunt Etty and cousins, Ella, Eric and Florrie, were from mother's side of the family and lived in Leeds.

Tom Blacow and myself were very good friends but sometimes we got into mischief. My father rented a field called 'The Frounts', where he kept one or two horses. A small bridge crossed a stream to the field and at the top of the field, on a slight rise, stood a barn. One day, unbeknown to my family, Tom and I went to play there. Outside the barn were the smouldering embers of a wood fire. Someone had been burning hedge clippings. We found some pieces of string and dipped them into a tar barrel we found nearby. We dangled the strings over the hot ashes and they alighted. We stupidly ran into the barn with the burning strings and before we knew what was happening, the barn was ablaze. I can't remember how the fire was extinguished but I do remember father was very angry when he found out about it. My father was a very gentle man and would never hit us but we were forbidden to go anywhere near the barn again, unless we were accompanied by an adult.

Frounts Barn in background with left to right - Walter Tatham's father, the boy on horse is an Oversby, father James Fisher, Walter Tatham and Richard Thornton. Richard was related to the Thornton brothers who built All Saints Church, Burton-in-Lonsdale in 1870

There being no television or radio in those days we made our own pleasure and one of these was to go with my parents, either to Clifford Wood or Black Wood, on the Wrayton Road, to watch the teams of horses hauling the great heavy logs. The horses were owned by a family called Green, who were timber merchants.

In 1909 there was a competition, sponsored by one of the leading newspapers to find the first person who could fly solo across the English Channel. A small biplane flew over the Town End of the village and it was so low, almost touching the roof tops. The pilot could be seen quite easily in the open cockpit. It caused quite a stir in those days. We discovered later that it was Louis Bleriot. This was after he had successfully flown solo over the English Channel on 25th July 1909, between Calais and Dover and was the first person to do so.

Our carefree days ended quite suddenly on 10th November, 1910. My father had a little boxing and wrestling school behind the 'Hen and Chickens' and many of the young men in the village came round there to train, including a young man called Walter Tatham, who weighed almost twenty stones. He challenged my father to a wrestling match. My father was a slim built man but nevertheless, he accepted the challenge. Tragically, he died of a heart attack during the bout. We were devastated. The funeral took place on Wednesday, the 23rd November, 1910 at All Saints Church, Burton-in-Lonsdale, followed by internment in the churchyard. He was thirty-four years old. I was six and Agnes was eight. I have no recollection of an inquest but probably I was too young to understand. I do, however, remember the stark reality of the tragedy and the feeling of great shock and sadness. My father was gone. He left money in trust for Agnes and myself and two trustees were appointed. They were our uncles, Harry Fearn and John Fisher. Mother had money in her own right. Things never seemed the same after that.

Being alone with a business to run and two young children to care for, my mother became friendly with Jack Wilson, a village resident slightly older than herself. He came from an old Burton family and had served as a soldier in the Boer War and used to be a regular at the 'Hen and Chickens' when father was alive. He persuaded her that Australia would be a good place to make a new start. They were married late 1911. Mother sold the 'Hen and Chickens' and preparations were hurriedly made for the journey. During these preparations Agnes and I were sent to a family in Masongill. I suppose it was to keep us from getting under their feet but I really hated those days.

At last, all preparations were made. Everything to be taken was packed into wooden crates. Mother insisted that we included in the luggage her set of Charles Dickens works, the family Bible and her precious mandolin, an instrument which she played with great enthusiasm. She often played and sang to us. I was allowed to take my very special cricket bat with me, which had been given to me by Grandma Crummock before we left. It had belonged to a Yorkshire and England cricketer who was lodging with my grandparents in Leeds. The back of it was covered with the autographs of many of the famous cricketers of the time and he was discarding it for a new bat. Mother had the bat shortened for me and rounded at the bottom. I was so proud of it!

14

Main Street, High Bentham about 1910   *Bernard Williams*

Town End, Bentham about 1910 with a dustbin cart on the right   *Bernard Williams*

Everything was loaded by Walter Tatham into the horse and trap taxi to be taken to Bentham Railway Station, two and a half miles distant. We left behind our lovely home with its sad memories and were whisked away, bag and baggage by train down to the docks at Tilbury where we and our precious belongings were stowed aboard a P & O Liner of about twelve thousand tonnage.

We had a reasonably pleasant journey with nobody ill. What should have been an exciting adventure for us was spoiled by Jack's drinking. He was frequently under the influence and bad tempered. Agnes and I kept out of his way as much as possible and occupied ourselves by making paper boats which we sailed down the channels when the decks were being swabbed. We were always sent packing by the crew if we were caught. There were other children on board and we all played together.

The journey took eight weeks. We sailed round Africa and the Cape of Good Hope. For some reason, we didn't go through the Suez Canal. I don't know why and I can only assume that the toll for passage was too high.

We landed safely at Sydney, in the Australian summer of 1912 and travelled immediately up country to Cottamundra.

A Peninsular and Oriental mail-steamer at an Australian wharf, with an Orient liner moving into position. Coloured streamers were bought before embarking and thrown over rails and people below caught hold of them and ran alongside boat until they snapped!
1st class single £100-£150 to England, 3rd class £38-£45 to England. *Photo 'The Argus' Melbourne*

Chapter Two
LIFE IN AUSTRALIA

We stayed in Cootamundra for a couple of days and then on to a sheep and cattle station further up the Queensland line and quite near a little place called Limbri, where Jack started clearing scrubland for a man named Mr Dorrington. He was paid so much for every acre cleared.

Our home, like most of the homes in that area, was made of corrugated tin with wooden supports, if you were lucky enough to find timber. These houses were built on stilts, firstly, to keep them reasonably cool and allow any air to circulate and secondly, to deter pests.

Our only water supply was collected from the tin roof in a large tank outside the door. The rain showers were few and far between so every drop of water was precious. We had not been living there long when I was sent out one night to fetch a can of water from the tank and it was then I had my first encounter with a poisonous snake. Inadvertently in the gloom I trod on it. I was terrified and luckily for me so was the snake, for it slithered off into the undergrowth.

It was soon after that there came a violent thunderstorm with not much rain but fierce lightning. A poor horse which was tethered to a metal clothes line was struck down and killed.

Life in Australia in those days was very primitive. Our home consisted of two rooms: a living room, a sleeping room and a veranda. Mother and Jack had the sleeping room, Agnes slept in the living room, whilst I enjoyed sleeping on the veranda. The nights were very warm and I found it the best place to be.

The only means of lighting was tallow candles. Later, we progressed to hurricane lamps and this was the form of lighting throughout my stay in Australia.

We had no proper toilet facilities, having only a plank to sit on over a trench, which could be a hazardous experience as there were so many poisonous snakes around.

All the household chores took place in the living quarters. Mother did all her cooking in a very large cast iron pot which she suspended over hot wood embers. There was no coal. Sometimes to assist cooking, embers were piled on the lid. Meat was cheap, so we had plenty of it and we ate porridge every morning for breakfast. Damper (unleavened) bread was baked in the pot every day, occasionally with baking powder.

Melons (water and rock), peaches, nectarines, plums, grapes (black and white - also used for wine), cherries and pears were plentiful in the season and blackberries and mushrooms were gathered in the wild for short periods after rain. Potatoes were difficult to grow or non-existent, so pumpkins which were plentiful were used in their place. We grew outside tomatoes, cucumbers and corn on the cob. On the whole, we had a very healthy diet. Mother was a good cook and made us delicacies, such as pumpkin and other jams, although sugar was hard to come by.

During the 1914-18 war, the Queensland sugar growers hoarded up the sugar until they could get a better price for it. At this time I gave up sugar in drinks and have never taken it since. Some sugar beet was grown but the taste was inferior. Perhaps there are better ways of refining from beet nowadays. Some people used syrup as a sweetener, or honey. Sweets were scarce and chocolate was unknown.

The wealthier farmers employed Chinese men to do large scale gardening. They maintained that these men were far superior gardeners to any of the white men they had employed. They were provided with money for seed and irrigation and grew fields of tobacco and lucerne, as well as runner beans, spring peas, wheat, maize, millet (the branched tops were used to make brooms), water and rock melons, pumpkins and plums. Grape vines also did well. For their labours they were given a share in the profits. Being friends of one of these farmers, we were invited to stay. Agnes and I had been watching a particular Chinese man tapping melons to see if they were ripe. He did this by taking out a small plug of melon to test and then putting it back. So we thought that we would have a go. When he caught us busily plugging his melons, he chased us all the way back to the house where the farmer's wife hid us under the bed. He was brandishing a knife but when I look back, I'm sure it was only in fun! Orchards were planted but were never successful.

I was eight or nine years old when I was given my first bike. Although it was a broken down effort and certainly not meant for distance travel, it was my pride and joy and I spent many happy hours riding it, after a few initial tumbles.

Between the ages of eight and fourteen, we hardly ever wore shoes except on special occasions. Once in a while, mother sent to Sydney for our shoes and often when they arrived they were a bit on the small side but nevertheless, we had to wear them. They had been bought so that was that! Later, hobnails were added to make them last even longer.

During our first four years in Australia, Agnes and I went to a little school a few miles distant. It was a small tin building on stilts and was nicknamed 'The Tin Tabernacle'! Each family contributed towards its upkeep. We were taught by a very nice Convent girl called Miss Giles, who had absconded from the Convent after taking her final vows as a nun. There was a big write-up in the papers at the time. Her boyfriend visited her at the school from time to time. The older children were taught by a German gentleman who was nearing retirement.

We walked to school each day. School hours were between nine in the morning and four in the afternoon, five days a week. We were taught the three R's, a bit of geography and lots of history. Agnes had a pet lamb which went to school with us. It would shelter under the building until we came out at lunch time. Then it would emerge to play, retreating to its shelter until home time. It was a merino and of course had a lovely thick fleece.

We took our lunch, which consisted mainly of sandwiches, usually mutton and a bottle of water, or milk in winter, with us to school and one of my most vivid memories was dashing out at lunch time with the rest of the children to a huge boulder a short distance away. It was covered with large shining crystals, more or

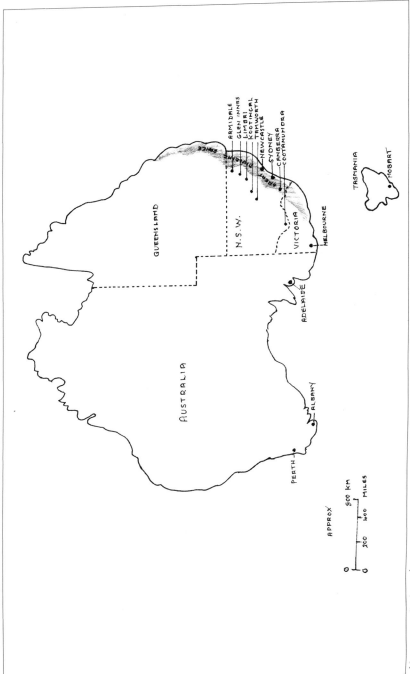

Map of Australia drawn by June Fisher showing relevant places

An old Settlers home similar to the one Jim and his family lived in - sketched by Robin Oliver, Australia

Limbri Railway Station, New South Wales, Australia, around 1918.

less six sided and about two inches long. Pieces that became detached sparkled like diamonds. We were told that their presence indicated tin or perhaps some other metals which were in the area. They were of course quartz (silica dioxide). That boulder was very special to all of us.

We had many friends at school and those days were some of our happiest. I remember a family of Irish children at school, that's if they weren't playing truant, called Cleary. Their father used to sit on the veranda smoking and talking to all and sundry, whilst his poor wife did all the work. Our young Convent girl teacher lodged with them. All the children at the school were Catholics. Agnes and I, being Protestants, were the odd ones out but everyone was friendly.

The game we played most often was cricket. I loved the game and used a piece of wood as a bat. Sadly, my special bat, along with mother's mandolin mysteriously disappeared soon after our arrival in Australia. I suspect Jack sold them but mother never mentioned it.

I was about nine or ten when I suddenly became very ill. Mother was very worried. The nearest specialist was in Tamworth, fifty miles away. The charge for bringing out a doctor or specialist was £1 per mile and £100 in those days was an awful lot of money. Jack was still on his drinking binges and our funds were dwindling fast, so mother decided she would take me to Tamworth. Horse and trap were our only means of transport and after I had been carefully wrapped and made comfortable, we set off on the very rough fifty mile journey. The specialist diagnosed rheumatic fever. He prescribed a thick, black paste to be smeared on my back and chest before I was swathed in cotton wool. We arrived home safely, although I don't remember much about the journey. I do remember, being in bed cocooned in cotton wool, with sweltering temperatures in the hundreds and mother turning me over every half hour. I was too weak to turn over by myself. This seemed to go on for a month or two until I miraculously recovered. We didn't see the specialist again.

It was about this time in 1914, when I was ten years old, that the Prince of Wales came to visit Australia. I remember people talking about it at the time. He travelled up to Queensland on a single track railway. A single light engine was connected to his private carriage, with a second engine at the back for protection in case of explosives on the line.

On 1st August, 1914 Germany declared war on Russia and on 3rd August, Germany declared war on France. Britain declared war on Germany on 4th August, 1914. Germany faced war from Russia in the east and from France, Britain and Belgium in the west. Being so far away from the war at the age of ten, I remember very little about it.

In 1918 the Australian troops returning from Europe were not allowed to be put ashore in Perth because the authorities thought they would bring in the black fever which was rife in Europe at the time. After twenty-four hours waiting on board the troops decided to take matters into their own hands. They lowered the lifeboats and rowed themselves ashore.

After four years clearing scrub for Mr Dorrington, our next move took us to a place about half a mile from Limbri Station. Mother and Jack bought 'Dorralma', a small farm and fenced it in. A river ran nearby but would sometimes dry up in the heat of summer leaving small pools here and there. The farm was sparsely stocked with one cow, two or three sheep and a few hens. Adjoining was a small field where we grew corn on the cob and wheat.

We were often troubled by snakes. The death adder, like a pink lizard, lurked on inaccessible ledges and even came into houses. There was an olive snake. Tiger snakes and brown snakes were deadly. The eastern tiger snakes would huddle together in a kind of bunch, but the deadliest of all was the windora in the outback. We also saw many scorpions. I once saw a huge snake slithering through wire netting and leaving its paper thin skin behind it, which wafted gently in the breeze long after its owner had gone.

When the river was full, I used to fish for catfish, which sometimes reached anything from five to six pounds in weight. They had poisonous barbs on their whiskers, so great care had to be taken when removing the hook. The bait was fresh water shrimps or one inch grubs, which we extracted from under the bark of rotting wood. Home-made lines were used and pieces of cork for floats.

Other fish caught were blackbaits weighing about half a pound and bluish in colour. Sometimes we caught fresh water cod. If the fish were plentiful, mother salted them down, as there was no means of refrigeration at this time. I also did night fishing, setting up several lines and leaving them until morning when I would dash along to see if I had caught anything.

I used to go swimming at night. I had learnt to swim at a very early age and became quite good at it. Whenever I had a break from chores or school, I would dash to the nearest water to swim. It was an excellent way of keeping both clean and cool. We didn't have bathing shorts, so we kept clear of the girls! Of course, if there was a swimming gala, shorts were worn.

Sometimes we had mini monsoons lasting about a week. Then the rivers were full. Pools formed everywhere and everything grew with great rapidity. It was in one of these moist periods between the long drought that I first noticed the bees drinking from the puddles. They all left the water vertically, some rising very high in the air and flying off to great distances. The ones which rose only a short distance, flew only short distances and I found I could follow them and find their nests in the hollow trees, which had been ring barked. I would go home, look for a four gallon kerosene tin and clean it out. Then, I would go to the nest taking with me my small axe, which I called my tomahawk and the kerosene tin. I covered my head and arms with old socks to protect me from stings, cutting small eyeholes. My legs were bare and were often stung unmercifully. The whole of the nest was hacked out with my tomahawk and dropped into the kerosene tin. When I reached home, the contents were transferred to a clean linen bag and left to drain into a basin. I used to make my own jam jars from Jack's empty beer bottles by dropping a red hot metal ring over their necks, then plunging the whole lot into cold water. The neck broke cleanly away and I filed round the edges to make them safe to handle. Mother and I filled them with honey, covered them with greaseproof paper and sold them for four pence a jar. The honey was aged by its colour. Dark honey was four to five years old, whilst light was less than a year. Native bees were small and made smaller nests. They produced only about half a pint of very rich, very sweet honey of excellent quality.

If the rivers were low and the fish weren't biting, someone would go up stream a way and stir up the water with a shovel specially taken for that very purpose. As the brown, muddied water travelled down stream, the fish were tricked into thinking, that flood waters were on the way and they would begin to take the bait.

Once, when I was about eight or nine years old and fishing alone, my bait kept disappearing mysteriously. Finally, as I hauled my line in, a huge black and red poisonous snake came lurching out onto the bank. Automatically, I picked up my tomahawk and in a flash cut the monster in half. What happened next was horrific! I knew that if I hadn't killed the snake, it would have most certainly killed me but I didn't expect its death to produce from the two halves, a crawling, milling bunch of young ones! I hurried off feeling quite sick.

On another occasion, I was more fortunate. I felt a tug on my line and knew there was something heavy on the end. It was impossible to haul it in but a nearby man, who had been taking an interest in my so called fishing skills, came to the rescue. We tugged together and pulled in a thirteen pound fresh water cod. I couldn't get home fast enough to show mother my precious catch. Mother was delighted and salted it down to be eaten later.

As well as looking after our small farm, Jack continued to do contract work for Mr Dorrington, clearing scrub. I went to help him one day and trying to be a big man, I was wielding a big axe, when I misjudged my swing and drove the axe into my leg just below the knee. It cut right to the bone. We bound it up and mother was in a terrible state when she saw it. There were no doctors available, so it just had to heal as best it could. I must have had good healing flesh but still have the scar.

Mr Dorrington started off in a very small way renting land from the Government which he cleared, or got someone to clear and paying off the debt annually at £1 per acre. Gradually, he built up his acreage as more land became available, until he had an average sized sheep station of about four to five thousand acres, with one merino sheep per acre.

You had to put your name down in order to buy land and at this time many wealthy English companies were given the best choice. Poorer people had to make do with poorer land which consequently produced inferior animals which could never be sold and many of which died. Mr Dorrington was fortunate to have found good, available land.

He told the tale that before he was married, he only possessed one pair of shoes which were reinforced with hob nails to make them last longer. Once or twice a year dances were held in the wool sheds. On these rare occasions, he removed the hob nails for 'dainty dancing' and replaced them later!

After marriage, he and his wife had four children, George, who was a sickly child, Mary, Elsie and Kathleen. He had a shotgun for disposing of rabbits, foxes, porcupine and other vermin. The gun had such a kick that he had to press his back against a tree before firing.

I was eleven years old at this time and gave up school to do odd jobs for Mr Dorrington, such as chopping logs, feeding the horses and domestic animals and checking the perimeter fencing, which consisted of wooden posts drilled to take five bars of wire. If the wire became slack, it was cut and the slack taken out. A special implement was used to draw the wires together and they were then secured with a reef knot. I was never paid for this work but did it willingly. I also began to help Jack with the scrub clearing for pasture land, which was mainly for sheep although horses and some cattle were kept.

We used to set out early and winter mornings produced a silvery frost which dispersed rapidly in the early morning sunshine. At first, clearing scrubland seemed quite exciting. There was such a lot to see. Larger trees were ring barked, by cutting a ring round the base about one foot to eighteen inches from the ground. In the heat, the trees quickly dried out and died leaving them hollow inside. They were then easier to remove. Odd ones missed became homes for small animals and bees. There were several types of eucalyptus trees, including messmate, box tree, iron bark (extremely hard) and springy bark, blue gum, pear gum, marri, vate mottlecah and several others which I can't recall. The Emperor gum moth bred avidly in the gums, was quite large and a vivid red in colour. Wild river oak and apple thrived but the most profuse and hardest to kill off, were the prickly pear and the verbena which threw out long, very active suckers. These had to be broken several times with the back of an axe before they eventually died. I once remember throwing a piece of prickly pear onto a burning hot tin roof thinking that would be the end of it. To my surprise, against all odds it grew! Among the scrub, this plant grew so thickly that even a small dog couldn't get through. The only way to kill prickly pear is to smother it. As long as air can get to it, it will grow. It is quite edible if you know how to peel it without tearing your fingers to shreds!

The currajung tree was pale leafed and not high growing. Its sap was like milk and the cattle and sheep loved it. The higher branches were cut for fodder but the climber had to take care, because the branches were brittle and fragile. The trees regrew from the bottom. Once, I climbed with my tomahawk to lop some of the upper branches. One suddenly cracked and gave way. I fell to the ground, hurting my ankle which even now troubles me from time to time.

Snakes were abundant and great care had to be taken to avoid them. I loved to see the iguanas, some of them four feet in length, climbing the trees with young on their backs, but in all the years I spent in Australia, I only saw one koala. Sadly, they were sought out at night and shot as they rested in the trees. Their fur was highly prized and used during the First World War for airmen's jackets and helmets. Thankfully, the Australian Government realised what was happening before they became extinct and brought out a law forbidding slaughter of the koala. Even now, they are not fully recovered. Rabbits and foxes were everywhere and hares too, though not as plentiful. Rabbit made a nice supplement to our diet. Jack set many traps for rabbits.

Peel Street, Tamworth, New South Wales, Australia in 1918. Sacks of wool probably being pulled along in the cart by the team of horses.

ow distance
doth divide us.
And I'm far
across the sea
I wonder, yes I wonder
do you sometimes
think of me?

Old Christmas card sent to Jim's mother by V Giles (Jim's teacher - the young Convent girl in Australia).

There were some very poisonous spiders lurking in the undergrowth. They were not much bigger than the British spider but very venomous, hiding under leaves or in the hollow trees. They also liked the dark corners in our homes. There were ants of every kind, the bulldog ant being the largest and most vicious. Most of the flies seemed to be blood suckers and there were plenty of beetles and cockroaches. Butterflies abounded and were of every size and colour. There were scorpions and large hornets which built transparent nests in the lower bushes. Some of the termite hills were yards high!

The bird life was very similar to that in England. On the lowlands there were sparrows, swallows, swifts, house and sand martins, crows, owls and magpies, which were larger in size than the European ones. Eagles soared in the hilly regions. Mutton birds (nicknamed - butcher birds!), were scavengers the size of large thrushes. They were grey with black markings and were good imitators. There were also thrushes, blackbirds and starlings.

In springtime, the sweet scented honeysuckle grew everywhere with the wild dog rose sheltering the shyer flowers like primroses, violets, buttercups and celandines. Some of the eucalyptus trees had wonderful blossom and of course, the wattle perfumed the breeze with its profusion of yellow flowers. The scotch thistles took over every empty space in the spring and when they were ripe, their airborne seeds blotted out the sun, the air being so thick with them.

The scrub sheltered animals, like wallabies, during the daytime until evening, when they came out to feed usually on the cultivated patches of land and, needless to say, they weren't too popular with the farmers. Foxes and dingoes were also pests. I remember running home when I was about ten years old, to report that I had seen a dingo close by. Nobody believed me but when mutilated lambs were found strewn about, the adults had to take action. Dingoes only seem to eat the liver and kidneys of their victims. A trap was set for it by tethering a domesticated bitch on heat and then waiting for him to appear, which in due course he did! The poor thing was then shot but stock had to be protected. Bishops and missionaries were responsible for bringing most of the pests into Australia. They also brought the prickly pear from Africa. There were camels in Australia but only in the Northern Territories.

Foxes and rabbits became so prolific that the Government passed legislation demanding that as many rabbits and foxes as possible must be poisoned, as their numbers had now reached dangerous proportions. Inspectors were sent round to all farms and sheep stations and any farmer not complying with the new legislation was prosecuted.

After the trade in koala pelts became illegal, rabbit, fox and hare skins were a good replacement. I remember being sent to buy strychnine crystals at £1 for a small bottle. Raspberry jam was used and this must have been imported, as I never saw raspberries or strawberries growing. The jam was laced with the poisonous crystals and deposited in small, specially prepared furrows. Rabbits and foxes loved the jam. They died a rapid, painless death and were then skinned. I became quite proficient at this and could skin between fifty and sixty rabbits an hour. Foxes were more difficult to skin and had a foul smell about them. The pelts had to be entire with the tail intact. In the early 1900's and well into the fifties, it was fashionable for the wealthier ladies to sport a fox fur with the tail dangling. Another marsupial was the possum or opossum, as the early settlers used to call it.

The porcupine, another pest, was a favourite food of the Aborigines. It was baked whole in clay and covered with hot wood embers. Fruit gathered by those nomads was eaten unskinned. They claimed, and rightly so, that the best nutrition was in the skin. We didn't see Aborigines often, but there was one who appeared on the sheep station every sheep shearing time and disappeared immediately afterwards.

The Aborigines weren't the only ones who found porcupine to their liking. Foxes went to great lengths for this delicacy. A porcupine confronted, always curls into a tight ball and in no way can it be opened without serious damage from spines, but the clever fox found a way. He would roll the animal into a stream, where it would immediately open up. Sharp teeth were then sunk into the soft underside and that was the end of the porcupine!

We were always back from our travels before bedtime, mother not wanting me out in the scrubland overnight. Our stepfather's drinking became heavier and his temper became more violent.

One fateful day, when I was fifteen, Jack sent me out early to collect rabbits from his traps. It took nearly all day and on my return I saw the horrific sight of our dear mother, who had been cruelly shot and was lying in pools of blood. The smell of human blood in that terrific Australian heat turned my stomach. Jack owned two rifles, a .22 and a .28 calibre and with one of these he had killed our mother. The railwaymen who had heard the shots as they were working on the line nearby, tried to disguise the horror of it all by covering mothers lifeless form with sheets. Agnes was seventeen at the time and working as a home help for a wealthy family in Tamworth, fifty miles away. Thankfully she saw nothing of the tragedy.

I never again entered the house where mother was murdered and had no further contact with Jack. One of the railwaymen had no hesitation in taking me back to his home, where his wife and children helped me through the trauma which has never really left me. The family was called O'Shea and they were Irish emigrants.

Agnes could not come to the funeral. The son of the household where she worked had carelessly tossed some large logs onto the kitchen fire where she was standing. Sparks flew out and set her alight. She was quite badly burned and spent a while in hospital.

Mother and Jack being extremely short of funds, had somehow got the trustees to release our trust money. What hadn't been spent before mother's death was now to be used for Jack's trial. People in Limbri said he would not be found guilty of mother's murder, him being a Freemason.

Jack's trial took place in Sydney around 1919, the first part lasting over one month and using up the rest of Agnes's and my nest egg. We were now penniless. The jury then disagreed over the verdict and the trial was postponed for a fortnight whilst fresh jurors were found. The trial then continued for a further fortnight and Jack was found guilty of murder and sentenced to fourteen years imprisonment, of which he only served eight. At one time during the trial he became so agitated that he accused me of carrying out the murder. The railwaymen knew that this wasn't possible as I had been out all day and they were close by when the shooting took place. The strange thing was, those witnesses to the killing were never called to the stand.

It is hard to forgive a man for such an horrendous crime and I still search out reasons for this terrible deed. I know he had served in South Africa and had witnessed many atrocities which may have pushed him over the edge, causing him to drown the memories with heavy drinking bouts and during one of these binges, he killed an innocent victim.

Chapter Three
ON OUR OWN

Agnes never returned to Limbri and I began to build a new life with the O'Shea family. They were great. Mr and Mrs O'Shea were kindness itself and I almost came to regard them as my parents. They had two sons, Les and Mick and two daughters, May, who was the eldest and married, and a daughter younger than me. Les and I became close friends and remained so until I returned to England six years later.

Their home was a good sized bungalow built of wood. There was a long dining kitchen area, divided by a trellis up which black and green grapes were grown, three or four bedrooms and the whole lot surrounded by a veranda where the family slept during the heat of summer.

This was a railway company house, situated close to Limbri Railway Station, where Mr O'Shea was station master, dealing with arrivals and departures, selling tickets and helping with passengers, as well as organising length checks each day as ganger. The lengthmen rode up and down on a two man trolley checking the length. It was worked manually and had to be lifted off the rails when trains were due. It was a single track line running up to Queensland and down from Limbri to Tamworth, Newcastle and on to Sydney

There was a half mile tunnel next to Limbri Station and Les, Mick and I frequently used it as a short cut to the open scrubland on the other side. It really wasn't too dangerous as there were only two trains a day, one up and one down. Besides, there were little recesses in the sides of the tunnel where we could shelter should a train come.

Sometimes a small group of us would set out to clear scrub and on these occasions, for the sake of safety, we built suspended bunks, rather like hammocks. There was always plenty of wood around suitable for the framework. Each morning our bedding was rolled tightly and tied up.

One of our group couldn't be bothered to build a hammock or roll his bedding. Only sissies bothered with such things! He soon learnt his lesson when climbing into his bed roll after our first day's work. To his horror, he found he was sharing his bedding with a large poisonous snake. He was fortunate not to have been bitten. Bunk building became his priority after this scaring experience!

When clearing scrub we always made camp by a clear stream but never drank the water until one of the party had travelled up stream to make sure that no animal (usually a sheep) had met its untimely death in the water. A stream needs to flow at least a mile in order to clean itself.

One very early spring, two terrible storms, one from the south and one from the north met over Limbri showering the land with massive, jagged hailstones. They rained down with such force that they killed all the domestic fowl and most of the wild birds. Jagged pieces came through the tin roof leaving gaping holes. The ice was swept in a torrent down a nearby culvert and was trapped at the bottom forming a huge ice mountain. The one and only good outcome of this event was that the whole community had iced drinks for a fortnight!

I decided I must make some money to go and visit Agnes in Tamworth. Mr Dorrington said he had a job for me and took me out into the backblocks (wilderness) by horse to the wildest part of his land and left me by a stream to erect my own small tent. My job was to poison rabbits. He gave me a bottle of strychnine and left me to it. I stayed on my own for over a fortnight with only my recent frightening thoughts for company. I found I was beginning to talk to myself so had to give it up. I packed up my meagre belongings and trudged back to Limbri.

Mr Dorrington took pity on me and gave me my second job which was delivering and collecting mail over a ten mile radius. He had the one and only shop in Limbri. He sold everything you could think of: from food, clothing, hardware, kerosene and other necessities. He was also the postmaster. He had a son who was my age but was smaller than me. We became boxing partners and always trained in the brilliant Australian moonlight, the rays of which were so bright that you could read by their light.

I felt so proud when I was supplied with two good pack horses to do my postal job. Fortunately, I was used to handling horses and had learnt to ride at an early age. The horses had a special saddle with hooks to evenly distribute the weight so making movement easier. One horse was for the outward journey and deliveries. The saddle was then changed over to the second horse for collections on the way back. Mail was left and collected from boxes by the sides of the track.

One of the large sheep and cattle stations where I delivered mail had once belonged to one of the three pioneers who had come over with the early settlers. They were called Blaxland, Wentworth and Lawson.

When Australia was first colonised from the Queensland border down the east coast to Sydney, the area became over populated and the settlers hadn't enough space to grow crops for themselves and their animals. They grew lucerne (alfalfa) to make ends meet. Three or four crops were grown each year, the last crop being kept for seed which was sold to wealthy landowners to supplement the settlers' incomes. Lucerne is a clover like plant with dark blue flowers.

It was during this difficult time (1813), that Blaxland, Wentworth and Lawson, decided to extend the colony by forging a way through the Blue Mountains. They faced many hardships, having to make several attempts before finally achieving their goal. The three stalwarts had to combat venomous snakes, crocodiles in swampy areas and hostile Aborigines who, quite rightly, tried to protect their land. Hundreds of miles of scrubland had to be hacked through before they eventually arrived at the Blue Mountains. Here they found astounding beauty in the flora and magnificent caverns, so big they could almost house a city. The rich soil on the lower slopes produced gorgeous wattle trees shimmering with sweet scented, bright yellow blossom which we call mimosa. Eventually they found a way through the mountains to reach the rich lands beyond.

Forgive me, I digress. I enjoyed my postal job and felt very adult now that I was actually earning money. I was paid ten shillings per week. Soon I had saved enough to visit Agnes in Tamworth. I did this occasionally, buying a single rail ticket to Tamworth and walking the fifty miles back, which I did along the rail track. It was much easier on the legs than walking the roughly made, muddy roads.

It was soon after that I developed excruciating toothache and being in urgent need of a dentist, decided to make the fifty mile walk along the railway track. It was the one and only time whilst in Australia that I suffered from toothache. I got about quarter of the way when a single engine on its way to Tamworth pulled up alongside. The driver asked me why I was walking along the line and when I gave my reasons, he kindly invited me to ride with them in the engine and dropped me off just outside Tamworth Station.

I will always remember the warmth and smell of oil on the footplate. It was exciting! The juddering and rocking of the engine as it crossed the points, the fireman shovelling coals and the steam all around made the journey thrilling for me in spite of the toothache. On arrival, I quickly found a dentist and the offending tooth was extracted for the cost of two Australian shillings. There was a huge abscess at the base of the tooth. There being no antibiotics in those days, I just had to put up with the pain that followed, it took many days to subside.

After mother's death, the trustees wanted us back in England and offered to pay our passage but Agnes, being seventeen and the elder, dug her heels in and refused to go. She said we would go when we had saved our own fares. So that was that. We stayed.

My friendship with Les continued and at the ages of sixteen we decided to go into business together clearing scrub for Mr Dorrington. We were paid very little for this work, sometimes a little more if the acreage cleared had been very heavy going. We used to take provisions and go off into the wilderness for days at a time. Our provisions consisted of salted pork to boil and our water was carried in home made canvas bags, which were stitched together with a bottle top sewn into the top for easy pouring. They were porous of course and the slight evaporation kept the water cool. We also kept bread and other items in canvas bags. Because most of our food was salted, we drank gallons of water. We also drank tea without sugar or milk. Besides boiled pork, we lived on bread and jam. A canvas tent was our refuge at night. We sometimes burnt scrub but only at night and when the wind was in the right direction. We never let the fires get out of hand.

Les unfortunately introduced me to the smoking habit. I was sixteen and in those days of course we didn't know of its dangers and it felt very manly to be puffing away at our rolled cigarettes. I used to buy a two ounce tin of tobacco and put a slice of potato in there to keep the tobacco moist. I became so adept at rolling cigarettes that I could do it quite skilfully whilst galloping along on horseback.

It was during one of these excursions that we first spotted rocks with a difference. They were strewn about a low hillside and were very heavy. We realised they contained metal. After having sent samples for analysis, we found they contained manganese for the finest steel, silver, gold and wolfram, a very valuable metal used for lining rifles and guns. Les and I started work in earnest

31

between scrub clearing and by digging into the hillside and collecting the smallest densest pieces, we soon had a small load, just the right weight to be packed onto the horses. It was then carted over land to Limbri Station, where it went by rail to Newcastle, for analysis and smelting. We staked our claim immediately and fenced in the area. The analysis showed more silver than gold. One ton of ore produced six ounces of gold. We worked hard for two years, drilling two foot holes into the rock, packing in gelignite sticks and plugging the holes with scree to get a better explosion. When drilling by hand, water was poured down the shaft to keep it cool. A twenty foot fuse was then lit whilst we sheltered behind nearby rocks. Our bugbear was the means of transport. Horses couldn't carry large loads over rough country. The rail fare and the smelting costs came to more than the price of the metals produced. Two young sixteen year olds hadn't the means to acquire machinery and the transport we required, so sadly we had to give it up. A mine had to be worked constantly otherwise it would be lost to the Government.

Some men spent months alone prospecting for gold, especially up in Northern Queensland, which was very sparsely populated. One hermit prospector was found dead in his bunk, with the body of his dead dog tethered beside him. He had been dead for months.

After the 1914-18 war, in around 1920, an American company opened up our mine and found it extremely rich in manganese, there being an almost solid block into the ground. They took over many gold and coal mines, smelting and other industries.

I remember once when Les and I were scrambling over boulders looking for signs of manganese, we came across a large cave. We went in and as our eyes became accustomed to the gloom, we were very surprised to see many kangaroos in various stages of decay and the floor littered with kangaroo bones. We wondered at the time and I still do, if kangaroos, like elephants, go to their own graveyard to die?

I was now almost seventeen and had moved on to work at a much larger sheep station. I was still gold mining and scrub clearing when I first moved there. After giving the latter up and leaving Mr Dorrington's sheep station behind, I remained full time on the Anderson station for the next four years.

Mr Anderson was the wealthy land owner and a distant relative of one of those early pioneers and owned other properties up and down the country. He was away most of the time and had an Italian manager to run things for him. The manager lived with his wife and three children in the big house. They engaged a housekeeper come nanny, who was a young girl called Burns and a maid. I was engaged for outside work and lived mostly in a wooden hut in the grounds, although I still spent some time with the O'Shea's. I did my own washing and ironing, using a flat iron heated over the embers. My wage was again ten shillings a week and out of this I kept myself in food and clothing. I was given a small patch of land to grow vegetables (marrows and pumpkins) and for this I paid a small rent and any mutton supplied from the house, had to be paid for. I caught rabbits, hares and occasionally a wallaby, to supplement my diet.

Sometimes I was invited to the house to eat but always in the kitchen with Burns and the maid. Once a week I had to kill a sheep and dress it for the table. What wasn't used that day was salted down to be eaten during the week. These fat sheep were kept in a special pen. If anyone rattled a bucket, the dogs would have one of these poor creatures cornered and ready for slaughter before you could say, 'Jack Robinson'! They associated the sound of clanking buckets with sheep slaughter and knew they were always well fed that day.

A couple of pigs were kept and pig killing took place twice a year. Once, I was roped in to help the storeman whose job it was to do the pig killing. He failed to do the job properly and the poor pig ran squealing all over the place, shedding blood everywhere. In those days there were no abattoirs and all meat for food had to be killed on the spot and eaten immediately, or salted down. These killings were certainly not the most pleasant of jobs but were necessary.

The station covered four hundred thousand to five hundred thousand acres with approximately one merino sheep per acre, plus two hundred head of cattle and a couple of bulls.

I spent many hours crutching the sheep to prevent blow fly attacks. The sheep were sheared under the back legs and shoulders and treated with ucacine and tar as a preventative measure to stop maggots. Affected sheep always made their condition obvious by continually trying to bite themselves. The treatment was also used to stop infection after branding cattle. Branding was necessary because of thieving. I also spent time erecting high fences to protect the stock from dingoes.

Spring time was dipping time. It was a big undertaking, always done in the cool of the morning. We used Coopers' sheep dip. It was a cream coloured powder, which we made into a paste and added to the dipping water. Dogs collected the sheep into vast yards and each sheep was pushed under the solution before climbing out.

Merino wool is the finest in the world and shearing was a very important time of year. About twenty shearers arrived on the station, bringing their own chef and helpers (classifiers, samplers, balers, packers and rouseabouts). The shearers ran their own newspaper, which was called 'The Independent Workers of the World', initials IWW which we called, 'I won't work!' They had their own unions, had disputes like everyone else and sometimes went on strike. It was good to be able to read outside news, as the only news which came our way, was by word of mouth or the very occasional weekly paper.

Shearing sheds were built on stilts. If rain was imminent, the sheep to be sheared that day would be brought in from the pastures and put under the sheds. Shearers refused to shear wet wool. The sheep were kept in pens under the sheds and as each animal was required, the shearer came out of a side door to hand pick his sheep. Some sheep were easier to shear than others and naturally the shearer tried to pick the best. Besides being excellent at their job, they were also excellent at swearing, having a good variety of expletives, especially if they got a sheep which was bad to shear!

Merinos only produced one lamb and did not have shepherds like we do, to

Drafting merino rams on a sheep station - typical Australian scene.

Commonwealth Government photo

Old style bullock team carting wool-bales to a railway station.

Commonwealth Government photo

34

supervise the birth. Nevertheless, not many sheep died during lambing. Merino sheep have very wrinkly skins and are not easy to shear at the best of times. The situation was made worse during very dry seasons, when shortage of grazing caused the fleece to stop growing. When the rains came, the grass grew rapidly and the sheep began to feed. The fleece began to grow again with a crack or a break in the strands, caused by the food shortage. The shearers hated this kind of fleece. It blunted their clippers. Also, this wool was not as valuable. The better off farmers could hold this wool back until they could get a better price for it. Sometimes, the stored wool would absorb moisture thus weighing more and reaching a higher price. Many sheep died during these dry spells and it was the job of the hands to pull the wool from the dead animals. This was called dead wool and was sold at a very cheap rate. The carcasses were then burnt, if wood could be found to make a fire.

As soon as the fleece was shorn, a rouseabout (a young lad), threw the fleece onto a long table, where it was classified by the expert, who usually thought himself a cut above everyone else. It was then graded, first or second class. The rouseabout also had the job of dabbing tar on any cuts accidentally made by the shearers. He also swept up, including the skirtings from the fleeces (soiled wool). These were thrown into a pile and later washed after the shearers had left, to sell off for next to nothing.

When the wool had been sampled the fleeces were rolled and put into a press containing a large sack which held about sixty fleeces. The press was manually operated by turning a handle. This made smaller, neater bales. The sacks were then sealed by sewing with a large bodkin and then stencilled with class number and destination.

The shearers usually worked in rows and could each shear an average of one hundred sheep in a day, for which they were paid between one and two pounds. They worked hard for their money, but £10 to £14 a week in around 1920, was quite a substantial wage.

The wool was then packed on to large four wheeled bullock carts for its long, sometimes hazardous journey over very rough terrain. It took at least six bullocks to pull each cart. They took a while to train, were slow moving, but very strong. Their pulling power was necessary because any occasional rain caused the carts to become bogged down and needed the strength of these beasts to pull them out of their difficulties.

During shearing time I sometimes slept in the tent with the shearers. It made a pleasant change and it was good to have company.

I think there were only about three working dogs but they certainly knew their jobs, hardly ever missing to retrieve even one sheep at shearing time. Very rarely a sheep was missed. The following year it was obvious if one had been missed. There would be in the midst of the flock, what appeared to be a walking, solid bale of wool! It was a comical sight!

Once or twice a year, I had to take a couple of horses to Glenninnes, a border town near Armidale, about sixty miles away to the north of the Queensland border.

Mr Anderson had property up there and sometimes needed more horses. I rode up and came back by train. These horses, related to brumbies, were running wild and free for most of the year and being used only occasionally, were not properly hardened to the saddle. On one journey, the horse I was riding developed a sore back. I had to ride the second horse. Mr Anderson was annoyed about the horse's back but it wasn't my fault. They just needed to be ridden more often. I wore elastic sided boots for riding. They kept my feet reasonably cool but I never wore socks - only for best.

On these occasions, I usually stayed a month and lived in a loft over the garage. Mr Anderson and family went on holiday whilst I was there and I took care of his stock, kept the house supplied with wood for the fires and saw to perimeter fences. We always kept one horse back in the evenings ready for work the next day. Saddles were used on working and racing horses but quite often we rode bare back. I enjoyed my time on the Anderson Station and learned a great deal about sheep.

At this time, there was a brumbie half breed horse called, 'Carbine', after the carbine rifle. It was the fastest horse ever to run in Australia. Then it went over to America to race, fell ill and died. It was brought back to Australia and sent to a taxidermist for preservation and is now in a museum in Sydney.

I was always grieved at gelding time and could never understand why the stallions were not gelded at a much younger age, likewise, sheep and cattle. The poor animals were felled and tied securely, each leg tied down separately and were then gelded with an instrument called an emasculator. It was heart rending to hear the screams of these animals. I had a soft spot for them, especially the horses. I loved my dogs but I loved horses more.

Life wasn't all hard work and no play. After the shearers had gone, the sheds were cleared out and made ready for the annual celebration. The floor had been well polished from all the lanolin in the wool and was ideal for dancing. The women folk made sandwiches and cakes and home brew was provided. The dancing commenced to accordion music. You had to be quick off the mark if you wanted to dance with a girl and you had to look after her well, if you wanted to keep her with you for the evening. You see, there were six men to every girl and the men not lucky enough to get a girl partner, had to dance together. The dancing went on from half past seven in the evening until five o'clock the next morning.

Some of the men drank too much and before the evening was over, odd scuffles broke out but they didn't spoil our enjoyment. We danced quicksteps, fox-trots, waltzes, barn dances and the lancers. Three dances were held each year and one of these was a charity dance for the hospital at Tamworth.

After all-night dancing, the land owners thought it was a good opportunity, since we were already up, to send us off round the perimeters with salt licks for the sheep and cattle. They were made up of dark green rock salt and were also enjoyed by the wallabies and kangaroos.

I took two horses with pack saddles and by noon, due to the lack of sleep, I was often exhausted. Having taken a packed lunch, I would sit in the shade tethering the horse to the tree, eat my well earned meal and would sometimes doze off only to wake and find myself in full sun but not the horse, which had cleverly moved round to keep in the shade.

At the weekends, horse races were held as a relaxation. I bought a horse occasionally during my early years, paying about ten shillings each time. Horses were cheap, especially during the long droughts when the farmers couldn't afford to feed all their stock. My favourite horse, which I bought from a distant farm for a little over ten shillings. I called 'Esmerelda'. She was a great horse and I think had some racing blood in her. She was lively and I used to race her at the weekends but never won anything, just enjoyed myself. Once, whilst riding Esmerelda, I leaned down to unhitch a gate, when to my great surprise, she leapt clean over the top of it, throwing me to the ground. I kept her until I came back to England in 1925 and was very sad to have to leave her behind.

A young man called, Anderson, came to teach at the school after I left and had replaced the retiring German who had been at the school for some years. Anderson was a great athlete and an excellent tennis player. He played for New South Wales when required, with the Doherty brothers who were two of the best Australian players at that time. He got us youngsters together and we formed a good tennis team. Six players went to each match and eventually I was one of them. Players were chosen by the ladder system. There were a number of people on the ladder and if you paid sixpence into the tennis fund, you could challenge the person on the rung above and if you won, you moved up. The players on the top six rungs played in the matches. I started playing tennis at the age of eleven and continued long after I came back to England.

The soil was too dry for grass to grow so we collected fine, red earth from the very tall termite hills. We covered our arms and faces as best we could, again using old socks and quickly carted away our spoils. This fine earth was then rolled into the tennis court, creating a grand, firm surface for play. Tapes were used to mark out the court.

We also played a lot of cricket and the retired German teacher was an excellent wicket keeper. Most of the games were just for fun. Some played rugby. I tried it once but didn't like it, so never played again.

Mr Murphy had a boarding house next to the station and had several daughters. Young Anderson was courting the eldest. I'm not sure whether or not they married but they were engaged when I left Australia in 1925.

I had several girl friends but never kept in touch with them when I returned to England. I remember being quite keen on Kathleen Dorrington and at the same time, Phyllis Morrison being sweet on me. She was a brilliant horse woman from Queensland and was a wonderful shot with a rifle. The Morrisons were big land owners and lived at Kootingal, near the Queensland border. There was some controversy about a railway being built across the border connecting up with New South Wales, unfortunately the wrong gauge had been used and passengers had to change trains at the border.

Christmas time on the Anderson sheep station was a little different from over here in England. For starters, Christmas presents were not exchanged and we didn't have a Christmas tree. We did however have a Christmas dinner with turkey. I was invited to the house for this meal but never dined with the family. My meals were always eaten in the kitchen with the maid and the housekeeper. Most of the hands used to get drunk. I drank wine occasionally and once got drunk after taking unseasoned homemade wine. We did not celebrate Boxing Day and there were no Bank Holidays.

In the summer of 1924, the trustees, Uncles John Fisher and Harry Fearn, through solicitors, contacted Agnes and myself, offering to find me an apprenticeship in England if we came back and asking Agnes if she would nurse Aunt Telly (Uncle Johns wife), who was an invalid. Agnes agreed, so we applied for passports. The authorities at first refused to issue them but eventually in the early spring of 1925, they agreed and arrangements were commenced.

We travelled up to Sydney by train and stayed in a small hostel, whilst details were finalised and having time on our hands, decided to see some of the local sights.

A Sydney girl, who was a relative of the Cleary family who lived in Limbri, took quite a shine to me and accompanied us on several journeys. We sailed the short distance to Manly, which was quite a popular resort. One of the finest zoos in the world occupies most of this rocky peninsula. Animals roamed free in their natural surroundings. It was a joy to see. I suppose it was one of the earliest natural zoos to be created. We visited Beachy Head at the entrance to Sydney Harbour.

One end of Sydney Harbour Bridge, in course of construction. This shows about one-seventh of the total construction. Cost £4,217,000 (British tender accepted). The central span was to be 1,650 ft long which was 650 ft longer than any other arch bridge in the world at that time.

Commonwealth Government photo

Many suicides took place here and often pieces of jewellery were found at the base of the cliffs. Sydney's Harbour is supposed to be one of the most spectacular in the world. They were starting to build the bridge at this time and we were later told that many suicides took place from the bridge itself.

At last, everything was organised and we were ready to sail. The girl who had accompanied us (sadly I can't recall her name), was sad to see us go and gave me a gold signet ring with her initials, as a keepsake. I didn't want to accept it but couldn't hurt her feelings. We never kept in touch.

We were only allowed to bring out a small amount of money. I had ten pounds and Agnes a little more.

A poem that I remember out of a book called 'Saltbush Bill, JP'; by AB Patterson, published in 1917 by Angus & Robertson Ltd, Sydney, which sums up these years I spent in Australia.

PIONEERS

They came of bold and roving stock that would not fixed abide;
They were the sons of field and flock since e'er they learnt to ride,
We may not hope to see such men in these degenerate years
As those explorers of the bush - the brave old pioneers.
'Twas they who rode the trackless bush in heat and storm and drought;
'Twas they who heard the master-word that called them farther out;
'Twas they who followed up the trail the mountain cattle made,
And pressed across the mighty range where now their bones are laid.
But now the times are dull and slow, the brave old days are dead
When hard bushmen started out, and forced their way ahead
By tangled scrub and forests grim towards the unknown west,
And spied the far-off promised land from off the range's crest.
Oh! ye that sleep in lonely graves by far-off ridge and plain,
We drink to you in silence now as Christmas comes again,
To you who fought the wilderness through rough unsettled years -
The founders of our nation's life, the brave old pioneers.

High Street, Bentham 1925

40

Chapter Four
BACK HOME TO ENGLAND

We sailed from Sydney in March 1925 and our first ports of call, were the North and South Islands of New Zealand, about six hundred miles from Australia. We took on a large cargo of apples intended for England. We stayed a couple of weeks between the two islands and then sailed on to Hobart, in Tasmania. I was very impressed by the neat English type houses, the Hansom cabs and the temperate climate. We stayed only about three days. The next stage of the journey took us back to Melbourne, in South Australia and then round to Adelaide. Next, we crossed the Great Australian Bight, where I suffered with sea sickness for over a fortnight, staying all that time on my bunk. The cabins had four bunks and it can't have been very pleasant for the other three passengers who had to share with me over that fortnight. I honestly thought I was going to die. Agnes was not affected. Eventually, we docked at a little place called Albany, on the southern tip of Western Australia, the sands on the shore were like white sugar. It was a beautiful little place and we stayed there two days, sailing next to Perth, on the Swan River. This was the last Australian call and we stayed there several days. My sea sickness, though not as severe, still persisted every time we put to sea.

The next stretch of water to cross was the Indian Ocean. We saw flying fish, porpoises, whales and the most beautiful sunsets I have ever seen or am likely to see again. It was like sailing into vast rivers of gold. Everyone collected at the ship's rails to watch these glorious spectacles.

After two weeks we arrived at Durban in South Africa but because of a storm, had to spend twenty-four hours out in the harbour before we could dock. Suddenly, to my great relief, the sickness left me and did not return for the rest of the journey home.

Durban had the most beautiful beaches for swimming. It was a tidy looking place with most of the seafront houses faced with white marble. There was a good zoo in Durban, though not as good as Manly but with a greater variety of animals.

Apartheid was in force and white and black people were not allowed to mix or travel on the same buses. It was sad to see the slaves filling ships' holds with coal. Two planks were placed against the side of the ship, one for up and one for down and these poor men, carrying heavy skips of coal worked continuously in a never ending, never resting stream. A guard stood over them with a rifle and a foreman with a whistle blew shrill blasts at regular intervals to keep the rhythm going. It took three days to fill each hold with coal and some of these slaves fell exhausted into the coal where they slept until prodded awake by the guard.

A few days here and then on to Cape Town further south. I was feeling a good deal better now and beginning to enjoy the voyage. The ship docked about a mile or so from Cape Town and the only means of transport for non-walkers was by rickshaws, some carrying one passenger and some two. These rickshaws were operated by a Zulu tribe, who ran themselves into the ground. They were short lived, dying very young from pneumonia, caused by being saturated with perspiration through running all day, then catching cold germs from foreign (mostly European) passengers.

It was here that I stupidly lost my ten pounds. A man on board was offering to change our money into Krugerrands, which were more valuable. Each coin contained one troy ounce of pure gold. They were minted in South Africa and widely used by investors or speculators in gold. After handing over my precious money, I never saw him again. Agnes was livid. She said, "You ought to have had more sense than to trust him," and rightly so! Thankfully she still had her money.

Next, the long trek up the coast to the Canary Islands. The ship stood out in the bay because the usual harbour hadn't been dredged. Islanders came out in little boats to take people ashore and trade with the passengers. Fruit and other merchandise came on board in baskets on pulleys. Money for these goods was returned the same way. Everything was honest and above board. I couldn't buy anything or go ashore because I had no money.

The cargo for passage to England was stacked high in crates on deck, there being no room in the hold. There was fresh green fruit, oranges, bananas, tomatoes and grapes, all packed in wood chippings. Wines and cigars were also packed in crates and the whole lot guarded over night in case of thieving. I met a Scottish girl on board ship but it was only a passing romance.

At last, the white cliffs of Dover came into view amidst great excitement among the passengers and soon we were docking where we had set out from, fourteen years earlier, at Tilbury. The journey had taken between eight and nine weeks.

We were met by our Uncles, John Fisher and Harry Fearn. We were given the sad news that Aunt Telly had died whilst we were on our way home. I didn't think our uncles would have recognized us after such a long time but they did. Whether it was the luggage we were carrying or us they recognized, I'm not sure but they were very pleased to see us both. After the initial welcome, we caught a train for the twenty mile journey into London. Then by London Midland and Scottish up to Leeds. The last part of our journey was from Leeds to Bentham.

I remember walking up Station Road and thinking how narrow the pavements were, Australian pavements being almost as wide as the streets. There was a group of youths standing on the corner in front of the grocer's shop owned by C Knowles and Sons and I wondered how I would get by them all with my luggage. We turned down Main Street and on to Uncle John's house, Vale View, which was near the Low Bentham end. They made us very welcome.

In order to accommodate us all, our cousin, Frank, who was fourteen years old, had to share a huge double bed with his father and I had a single bed, in the large front bedroom. Agnes had the back bedroom. She buckled down immediately, making meals, washing and keeping house. Whilst there, I remember seeing an illuminated manuscript, kept proudly by my uncle, stating that he had attended Burton-in-Lonsdale School for eleven years and had never once been ill or late.

The dining room was at the back and once when Uncle John was having his

High Bentham Railway Station around 1900
'Buildings typical of most on the Skipton to Lancaster line, being 'mock' Tudor design. Note the station master and his staff with steam train entering station.
Canon John Bearpark

43

after lunch siesta, the cat, who was sitting in the sunshine on the windowsill, suddenly spotted a large fly sitting on Uncle John's bald spot and sprang into action. He didn't manage to catch the fly but landed neatly on Uncle Johns head giving him the fright of his life! Later, but not at the time, we often laughed about it.

Shortly after our arrival in England, my sister Agnes became ill with influenza and had to stay in bed. Our cousin, Agnes Fisher from 'Hill Cross', Burton-in-Lonsdale came to look after her. My aunt was a semi-invalid and suffered from bronchitis. She was always burning strange smelling substances and her house reeked of the fumes. She was also very strict with her daughter, who at that time was courting Tommy Preece. The courting had to be done secretly and if Tommy couldn't get to see Agnes, he always left pebbles on the windowsill, so that she knew he had been. When Agnes came to look after my sister, Tommy would always call to see her. My Uncle John said, "I'll put a stop to all this secrecy", and he allowed them time together in the front room before Tommy went home. My aunt finally had to accept that they were keeping company and they were married shortly after.

I remember during my first few weeks back in England in 1925, the circus came to Bentham. It was held in a field behind the 'Horse and Farrier'. Uncle John Fisher was keen to enter me in local competitions and I suppose it was his way of introducing me to people. Well, on this occasion, the circus master had a twenty foot whip, made from plaited cow hide and hair from the horse's tail. He cracked it once and offered a gold chain to anyone who could do the same. Uncle John pushed me forward to have a go. I surprised the ringmaster by cracking it twice whilst the whip was in the air. I received my gold chain but of course it was only imitation!

Agnes kept home for us for about eighteen months. She started courting a local man and they decided to go out to Australia together. Once in Australia, he deserted her, befriended another girl and returned with his new girlfriend to England. Agnes never returned to England, she married and had a lovely daughter, called Robin. Robin still lives out in Australia, she travels the world and last visited me in 1997.

Work was hard to come by and there seemed to be unrest. In 1926 there was a general strike to express solidarity with the coal miners who were campaigning against wage cuts. Large families and low wages made very poor living conditions and disease was rife. Servicemen and volunteers kept essential services running and the strike crumbled after ten days. The country was in the grips of depression.

Although my uncles had promised me an apprenticeship if I returned home to England, it never really materialised. At first I went out travelling with Uncle John who was venturing out into the clothier business, after serving a five year apprenticeship with Charles Garlick who had a drapery business in Bentham at that time, he started off in a room in his house and then rented a small shop down Station Road. His only means of transport was a motorcycle and he attached a sidecar to accommodate me. We had quite a few hair raising journeys and my work with him was short lived. I remember, once in a blizzard, I had to push the bike with Uncle John still on board, nearly all the way from Slaidburn to Bentham. I was exhausted!

Wenning Bridge & St Margaret's Church, High Bentham in 1920's   *Bernard Williams*

Footbridge over the River Wenning, High Bentham in the 1920's   *Stanley Wilkinson*

Bathing Pool, Bentham on River Wenning - Bathing hut used as a changing room and courting hut.
Bernard Williams

Dr Arthur James Troughton, seated in the drivers seat of his early Ford car, with solid tyre and wooden spokes. He was the first doctor to use a car on his rounds - previously used a horse.

David Johnson Collection

Eventually, I had to go on the dole. Those wanting work would trail down to the gas works each day. You had to be there before 10am to stand any chance and queue along the wall. Then a Welshman called Mr Owen, would come out of his hut, which he called his office and would pick those who he wanted to work for him. He would say, "I'll have you, you and you. The rest of you can go home!"

One day, I was lucky. He handed me a crowbar and said, "I want the top storey of the mill in Wenning Avenue dismantling." The roof was falling in and the other men below thought I was mad to climb so high but I had been used to climbing tall trees in Australia, so heights didn't bother me. I worked alone and had the sad job of destroying beautiful windowsills and a lovely pitch pine staircase. It seemed such a shame and waste but I just obeyed instructions. The stone, wood and debris was carted away in lorries by a team of men working below. When the building was reduced to the first floor level it was combined with the other existing mill. This took me about a month and I was finished.

I was also lucky enough to get odd jobs at the tar works, tarring roofs to keep out the weather, or mixing paints for the analyst, who was employed by the company. He proudly told me that he had been out in India and had employed a servant, for two pence a week and that he never once had to fasten his own shoes. Needless to say, his servant always did this for him.

Since my early mining days and exploits I have always been interested in mineralogy and decided to take a correspondence course on the subject. Sadly, I had to give it up. Being in and out of work at the time, meant I didn't have the money to carry on with the course.

In the midsummer of 1925 there was a Horticultural Show held at Burton-in-Lonsdale, with a Fancy Dress Parade in the afternoon, followed by a dance in the evening. I was persuaded to dress up as an Arab and won first prize. A girl I knew recognised me and asked if I would take her to the dance in the evening. She was nice and I readily agreed. We later met up and set off together. As we walked through the door, she promptly disappeared and I didn't see her again all evening!

In 1926, Dr Troughton organised a swimming gala on the River Wenning. The trainer was Wilcock Whittaker and of course I was roped in to swim. The swimming hut where we changed, also doubled as a courting hut. I found the water and climate very cold after Australia and caught a severe chill. Dr Troughton sent me to bed for a few days. On the day, Frank Sedgewick was the winner and I came second. I used to train regularly with Tom and Robert Guy and Jim Davidson. Tom was an excellent runner and would have gone far in the athletics world but alas one day, he went up Summer Hill, above Bentham, on his bike to collect rents. On returning a car crossed in front of him. The driver was turning into his lane. Tom hit the car at speed and was cast over Wenning Bridge into the river. He was killed instantly. Wilcock Whittaker our swimming trainer, also produced amateur dramatics in the Town Hall in Bentham. From the 1920's onwards the Society used to put on some excellent plays.

Uncle John's enthusiasm never waned on entering me for any swimming, running or other competitions. He invited me to join the cricket team and we had

Bentham Agricultural Show in 1920's, which was held down Station Road on the other side of the river bridge beside the River Wenning.

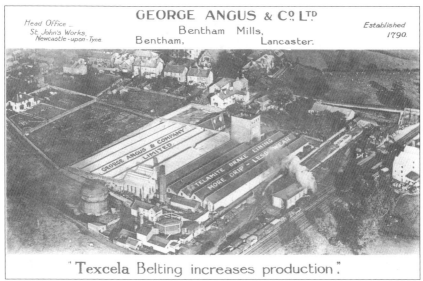

GEORGE ANGUS & C⁰ LTD

Head Office _
St. John's Works,
Newcastle-upon-Tyne

Bentham Mills,
Bentham,   Lancaster.

Established
1790.

"Texcela Belting increases production".

George Angus & Co Ltd aerial photograph used for publicity.

22 inch belt driving machine at George Angus & Co Ltd. Jim worked on this type of machine. See the rows of cops mentioned on left.   *Bernard Williams*

Men working in the weaving shed at George Angus & Co Ltd in the 1940's.   *Bernard Williams*

THE

BENTHAM WOVEN HOSE & BELTING WORKS

GEO. ANGUS & Cº LIMITED - PROPRIETORS.

Manufacturers of
·SEAMLESS WOVEN HOSE·STITCHED COTTON BELTING·
·HAIR BELTING · SOLID WOVEN ELEVATOR BELTING·
Speciality :
·COTTON CONVEYOR BELTING·

BENTHAM,   March 5th 1928.   19
LANCASTER.

This is to certify that the bearer, Mr J. Fisher,
has worked for us as a Belt Weaver for four
years. We have found him to be an efficient and
willing worker and he is leaving us of his own
accord.

GEO. ANGUS & CO., Ltd.

Reference given to Jim. Please note they have the years wrong. It should read he worked there for three years not four.

some good games. He was the secretary of the High Bentham Cricket Club for many years and we were in the first team. Once, when we went to Garstang to play, we won the toss and put them in to bat. They only made eleven runs. We only had to make twelve runs to win, which suited us down to the ground because we finished early and spent the evening at the cinema in Lancaster. The newspaper report said something about the two Fishers winning at Garstang. I also enjoyed and played a lot of tennis at this time.

Molly Bateson, the little girl I used to sing with when we were three years old, asked me to meet her in Green Lane (or 'Lovers Lane', as the locals called it), one afternoon. I went along and found her waiting for me with another girl. They had brought a lovely picnic, which we all shared and enjoyed.

I remember a sad incident, not long after my return from Australia, around 1926, Tom Fearn, Arthur Fisher and myself borrowed bikes and rode over to Morecambe for a day out. We arrived at the Town Hall and saw the sad sight of five dead fishermen, who had drowned when their boat capsized, being carried ashore and laid on the promenade.

At the age of twenty-three, in 1927, I saw my first total eclipse of the sun. Frank Dyson, the Astromomer Royal at that time set up his telescopes at Giggleswick, about twelve miles from Bentham. This was apparently the best viewing point.

I didn't go to Giggleswick but nevertheless had a wonderful view from Abours Barn which was on high ground between High Bentham and Burton-in-Lonsdale. Friends and neighbours from around Uncle John's house gathered and we all went up together. We viewed the eclipse through pieces of glass blackened with smoke from burning candles. The totality lasted about a couple of minutes and the air became extremely cold. It was very exciting!

Seventy-two years later, the south of England saw a total eclipse at 11.11am on the 12 August 1999. The north saw only a partial eclipse. We had the drop in temperature, but not the darkness.

The next job I had was with George Angus & Co, as a belt weaver. We used to weave cotton belts twenty-two inches wide, by a quarter of an inch thick. They were called endless belts for driving machinery. It took one thousand cops to feed the shuttles. Cops were wax tubes holding thread. At first, we were put on piece work as an incentive to get on with the job but as soon as we became efficient, some of us earning up to three pounds ten shillings a week, the management stopped piece work and put us all on a weekly wage of two guineas.

A new shed was build at this time for the weaving looms and although it wasn't finished, three or four men including myself had to work in there. There were no proper walls and we worked all one winter in the cold. We went to the management to complain but they always made excuses.

George Angus did provide us with some recreation when arrangements were made once a year for us to go and watch Preston North End play. We went by bus to Lancaster, then by bus again right to the football ground, all for half a crown. It was brilliant!

Towards the end of the twenties, the factory bought a new Rushton Lincoln engine. Mr Bush had always looked after the boiler and continued to maintain the new engine which he did with great pride, keeping it well polished and in good working order.

As the firm expanded, brand new weaving looms were bought and stacked ready for assembly in the belt race. Shortly after this, these new looms were broken up for scrap without ever being used. The only reason I can think of for this was the introduction of circular looms.

Unfortunately, none of the jobs were full time. We used to work a week and then have a week on the dole. This lasted for about six months but at Christmas there was always overtime.

Chapter Five

EARLY MARRIED LIFE AT GRASSRIGG AND THE QUAKERS

Uncle John Fisher was a Quaker and when I first came back to England he took me to Sunday Meeting and I saw Mary (Knowles) there but we didn't meet officially until about two and a half years later. I still remember clearly the first time I met and spoke to Mary in 1927, when I was on the railway bridge with some of my cousins who had come over to Bentham to seek out the girls. The railway bridge was a popular meeting place for young people in those days. We sometimes as a treat went dancing to Morecambe Pier. That day there was Edgar Fisher, whose father Tom and his mother farmed at Gallaber, in Burton-in-Lonsdale, Tom Fearn, Arthur Fisher and Agnes Fisher, who introduced me to Mary. My younger cousin, Annie Fearn was not with them. She later married Arthur Tustin, whose father was the Bentham Police Sergeant and owned one of the earlier Ivy Three, belt driven motor cycles.

My friends and I would go by early evening train to Morecambe and arrive back at Bentham Station some time after eleven. We danced the same dances as in Australia with two-steps, quick-steps, fox-trots and waltzes. Our favourite dance was of course, the lancers.

We galloped round in our circles so fast that the girls' feet flew off the ground into the air. They giggled and squealed and we all thoroughly enjoyed the experience. Whenever the MC announced 'the lancers', the girls were always first out of their seats.

I had seen Mary quite a few times coming out of George Angus & Co, where she worked in the offices but had never had the opportunity to speak to her until that night on the railway bridge. We took a shine to each other and courting commenced. Mary sometimes had to work overtime at Christmas and didn't finish until 11 pm. I would go and meet her from work and walk her home to Grassrigg, where she lived with her mother, Agnes and her sister, Margaret, who was three years her junior. She also had a brother George, who was the eldest and was away in Canada at the time.

In late 1922, Mary's father, Christopher Knowles built 'Grassrigg', up Goodenber Road, Bentham, where the family immediately went to live. Christopher became ill, with a kidney complaint and went into hospital, in Lancaster. It was claimed by the family, that he died there through negligence in 1924, at the age of sixty-four. I never knew him, although I understood him to be a fair-minded intellectual man.

When Mary and I were courting, we sometimes went to Sedbergh to stay with Mary's Aunt Maggie. At least that's where Mary stayed. I was farmed out to a room about a quarter of a mile away. Aunt Maggie was matron at Manchester Royal Infirmary and was a strict disciplinarian. Until we were married we were not allowed to sleep under the same roof. My sleeping quarters were above a shop in Sedbergh, the room being let out for bed and breakfast. After breakfast, Mary and I would meet up and walk for miles. We had some wonderful walks in those days, never tiring of the marvellous scenery around Sedbergh, with its steep fells and the glorious colour of autumn bracken against the clear blue sky. We walked along the crystal waters of the River Rawthey and listened to the songs of the skylarks high in the sky, a sound we hear much less of nowadays. Higher up the fells we occasionally heard the screech of eagles.

When I first attended Quaker Sunday Meetings, I found the silence strange, but refreshing and as each individual spoke, I found wisdom in their words and later enjoyed the peace and tranquillity of each Meeting. I found my Quaker friends to be honest, sincere and hard-working people and was amazed at the good that the Quaker Movement was doing throughout the world, both practically and spiritually. A lot of Mary's family were Quakers and I became a fully fledged member just before our marriage in 1930 and have never regretted it. There was always a good attendance at Meetings.

Some of the names that I remember from these times are: Charles and Mrs Ford (Charles owned the Ford Airton Pure Silk Mill at Low Bentham and at one time owned the early Abbot's Hall, now known as Mewith Head Hall. There the constant water supply was a crystal clear stream, which ran through the kitchen), Mr and Mrs Forrester, Mr and Mrs Philip Harvey, Geoffrey and Margaret Holmes, Frank and Edie Fisher, Edward Hutchinson, Annie Knowles, Mr and Mrs Reed, Dr Leslie and Dr Elizabeth Dowell, Mr and Mrs Townley, Mr and Mrs Sanderson, Margaret Knowles and Edgar Ramskill, Agnes Knowles, Mary, myself and Mr and Mrs Tapsell and quite a few others which I can't bring to mind. Christopher Knowles (Mary's father) was a staunch Quaker until his death in 1924.

One of the early Bentham doctors was called Dowe. His wife's father was a Quaker called Robertshaw and during the First World War, he did a great deal to rehabilitate the unemployed. One of the things he did, was to start up the allotments scheme in Bentham.

Mary and I courted for two or three years and were married at Calf Cop Meeting House, the day before Mary's birthday, 9th August 1930. Margaret Knowles, (Mary's sister) was bridesmaid and Mary was given away by Thomas Knowles. My best man was Edgar Ramskill. The reception was held at the Friends Meeting House, Main Street, Bentham. I was twenty-five and Mary was twenty-three. The man in charge at Angus Fire Armour Ltd, where Mary worked, was a Quaker called Mr Sowerby. He gave us a picture of roses painted by Maude Angell and it still hangs on my wall today.

We spent our honeymoon in Llandudno, hoping for lovely August sunshine but the weather was not good. We returned to Grassrigg, where Mary and I lived in the attic bedsitter. We did our cooking there, sharing only the bathroom and laundering facilities with Mary's mother and sister Margaret.

I was still smoking when I returned to England and Woodbines were tuppence for a packet of five. When Mary and I were first courting and in our early marriage, she always bought me a packet of 'Three Castles' for my birthdays and

Courting days - left to right - Jim, Mary Knowles, Margaret Knowles (Mary's sister) and George Knowles (Mary's brother) and of course Tinker number 1.

Wedding photo - 9th August 1930
Back left to right - Uncle John Fisher who gave Mary away, Agnes Knowles (Mary's mother), Margaret was bridesmaid (Mary's sister), Edgar Ramskill was best man (Margaret's fiancé).
Front - Mary and Jim with Ray Lancaster

55

Inside Calf Cop today with its peaceful beauty. (July 1999) *June Fisher*

Outside Calf Cop. (August 1999) *Anne Bonney*

at Christmas. They were handmade and one of the most expensive cigarettes on the market at that time and came in a flashy green packet. I was about fifty when I finally gave up the habit. It wasn't easy and I put on quite a bit of weight at first but that soon settled down and I became better off, both in health and in pocket.

Mary and Margaret bought a budgerigar. They were very fond of it and used to let it fly freely about the house. It was a greeny blue colour and very attractive. On sunny days the cage was hung out on the washing line so that Billy could benefit from the sunshine and fresh air.

One evening, I arrived home from work to find Mary and Margaret very distressed. Billy had somehow escaped from his cage whilst it was hanging outside. The cage door could not have been properly fastened. He could be seen perching in a large tree at the bottom of the garden and no amount of calling, would coax him down.

Night was falling and the girls thought that Billy would die, or be killed by other birds. The next morning, Billy could be seen on the overhead telegraph wire and I suggested that they might leave the cage, with open door on the wash house roof at the back of the house. When we looked out much later in the morning, we saw Billy fly down and enter his cage. I dashed out and closed the cage door. Hunger had probably attracted him to the food in his cage. Billy was safe!

Soon after our marriage, I saved up and bought a twelve foot by eight foot greenhouse, which I had seen advertised in the local paper. After about a year, some workmen came to do repairs at Grassrigg. As well as plants, I kept all my tools in there. I was in bed one night when I heard a terrific crash. The greenhouse had smashed up against the garden wall. The workmen had also put their tools in the greenhouse but had left the door swinging in the wind, causing the whole lot to collapse. Edgar's Uncle, Herbert Ramskill, helped me to put the remains together again, this time against the wall like a lean-to. It was a bit small but serviceable. One morning, whilst construction of the new lean-to was in progress, I went in to prepare a tomato bed and there before my eyes was a pale green egg a little smaller than a hen's egg. I found out later that a guinea fowl must have flown across the fields from the farm in the night, laid an egg and then returned home.

One afternoon, whilst I was working in the garden at Grassrigg, I overheard two farmers haggling over the price of a cow which one of them had for sale.

There was a stile at the bottom of our garden and when a provisional agreed price was reached, one of the men would climb up on the stile ready to shake hands and complete the deal. Unfortunately the deal was never completed and throughout the whole of the afternoon, first one and then the other climbed the stile hoping to seal the bargain which after hours of negotiating, never took place.

The stile was always well used. The field beyond it was a favourite place to walk dogs, take a short cut home or even to walk hand in hand with your sweetheart.

One gentleman was frequently inebriated and the stile was never easy to negotiate. He found it a great trial, especially as he needed to cross it to get home.

Try as he might, he could not climb over. First, he would manage one or two steps, roll off and start again. After several attempts, he would turn round and try a backwards ascent. Fortunately, someone always seemed to come to his rescue. He would be either pushed, or pulled over the dreaded stile thus ensuring his safe return home.

We had one of the first radios in Bentham. It had two accumulator batteries, a twelve volt and a four volt. It was built in Holland and we bought it from the Craven Wireless Shop in Clapham, which was owned by a German gentleman called Mr Petty. His assistant was called Mrs Rodgers and they also had a workshop in the Ingleborough estate grounds. There was a sealed unit in the radio and if ever it developed a fault, the part had to go back to Holland for repair.

We had to have a very long aerial across the garden at Grassrigg and it was attached to a twenty foot pole. One night, the aerial blew down in a storm. The wire had snapped at the top of the pole. Mary didn't like me scaling the pole to fix the wire but I managed, with a certain amount of effort to make a successful join. Mr Petty later bought a shop in Main Street, Bentham and called it, 'The Craven Wireless'.

In my early marriage, I remember a small, private biplane landing in the fields just behind Grassrigg. The young pilot had run out of petrol. He left his plane in the field overnight. When darkness fell, Mary, Margaret, Edgar and myself, set out across the fields to have a look at it. We were all very excited. To be able to see a plane at such close quarters created a great deal of interest. On arrival, we found many others gathered round. The next morning, after refuelling the pilot took off. It was an event talked about for ages.

In the mid-thirties a flying circus used to visit Bentham. It was held in a field down by the River Wenning, across from the sewerage plant. There were two small biplanes with open cockpits and the pilots were offering to take people up for a fee, which was about £5. I remember a pretty young girl was given quite a few flights. I think she had taken quite a shine to one of the pilots!

Chapter Six
WORKING FOR CHRISTOPHER KNOWLES

By this time, 1930, I was working for Christopher Knowles whose shop was on the corner of Station Road and Main Street. It was a huge shop selling a variety of merchandise. On the ground floor, every kind of grocery was sold, everything being measured out and packed by hand.

By rail, both white and wholemeal flour and corn came in white, cotton fifty pound bags. It was sold by us to confectioners and cafes in ten stone jute bags. Sugar came in fifty pound jute bags. Bramley apples came from Ireland, packed in straw in large barrels. Syrup, treacle and cow treacle also came in barrels. Dried fruit came by rail in beautiful wooden boxes. All dried fruit had to be cleaned. It was put through running water in a machine turned by hand. The turning was then speeded up, to spin dry the fruit, which was then turned out on to a long table, where the bits of stick and debris were removed. Occasionally, we even found specks of bird droppings but everything left the shop in perfect condition.

The syrup and treacle barrels were tapped and the contents sold loose in earthenware containers, which were weighed before they were filled. The containers were charged for, unless customers brought their own.

Yeast was bought in seven pound blocks and was sold off a few ounces at a time. Every kind of spice was bought wholesale from the cities. Potatoes came by road from Cumberland, in one hundred weight sacks. When the potato stocks began to dwindle, I used to drive to Preston on Saturday mornings to buy more. The cheeses arrived up to sixty pounds in weight, were labelled and taken to the cellar on to long trestle tables housing sometimes as many as sixty cheeses. They were turned each morning by me after I had lit the boiler at 6 o'clock. The boiler heated all three storeys but not the store houses down King Street. Sides of bacon, butter and eggs, were kept in the coolness of the cellar. We always kept cats on the premises to deter any mice.

On Saturdays, I collected coke from the gas works and shovelled it down a shute next to the boiler. We also bought tar in four and five gallon tins, mostly for our farmer customers.

At this time, the only means of transport for deliveries was a horse and cart. The horse called 'Dinah', was stabled down King Street in cold weather but set loose in fields up Goodenber Road, High Bentham, belonging to Christopher Knowles & Sons, at other times. The fields were cut at haytime and the grass stored in King Street, for Dinah's winter fodder. It was Bob Foster's job to look after the horse but sometimes in winter, when Dinah had to be bedded down for the night, I did the honours and fed her bran mash. I always enjoyed attending to Dinah and got on well with her but she sometimes bit Bob for no apparent reason because he too always treated her well. Many of the Bentham children got to know her because Bob would often allow them to ride on her back as he took her up Goodenber Road to graze overnight in the fields there.

The rest of the store houses down King Street were used for storing potatoes as well as provender, corn, bran and Uveco (trade name for flake maize). One thousand sacks of potatoes each weighing one hundred weight were delivered by lorry. If sales were slack, I used to go selling potatoes on Saturday mornings round Ingleton, Low Bentham, Burton-in-Lonsdale and Clapham.

The cost of a one hundred weight bag of potatoes, if tipped out was four shillings. If the potatoes were purchased in a sack, then a sixpenny ticket was given to be redeemed off the price of the next load. For one pound glass jam jars, we paid four pence per dozen - for two pound jars, sixpence per dozen and for pint bottles, one penny each. Stoneware bottles, jars and other containers had their values printed on the bottom and if returned, we paid that price.

On the same floor as the groceries, in a far corner, were kept block salt, barrels of syrup and treacle and drums of paraffin and linseed oil. There were two types of paraffin, one for lamps and one for cooking. There were also two kinds of linseed oil, the kind boiled for paint and the other used raw for animals. Large bottles of vinegar were also stored there.

Some of the containers were made at Burton-in-Lonsdale, the heavier, larger bottles being encased in baskets, with handles for easy carrying. At the pottery, a man called Squire Taylor, used to sit on the floor cross legged each day, weaving baskets of willow round the one and two gallon bottles. The pottery was owned and worked by Richard Bateson and his team of workers. We were always amazed by his skill in fashioning pots on his treadle worked potter's wheel. It was fascinating to watch the clay being cut from the clay pans, then being taken in to be wedged (this is when a block of clay is cut into two large triangles using wire and pounded on a solid surface so that there is no air bubbles trapped in the clay which could cause it to explode in the kiln - then cut into pieces). After being weighed, the pieces were sent up to Richard, who threw them on to the wheel and all too soon, perfect pots would appear. They were then put on shelves to dry out, later to be glazed and fired in the kilns. In the early days I believe there were thirteen potteries at Burton-in-Lonsdale.

On the upper floor of C Knowles & Son, crockery was displayed and sold. Aunt Lizzie, Mary's father's sister, was in charge here and she, bought only the best. Customers climbed the beautiful staircase, to view high-class tea and dinner services with all kinds of other china, tastefully displayed on the long shelves. The crockery arrived in huge crates, which were hauled up to the top floor through double trap doors by hand pulleys. In the same way, provender, corn and Uveco, were hauled up to the top floors of the storage buildings in King Street. Some farmers liked mixed animal feed and this was done with a shovel on the floor and bagged up into one hundred weight sacks. Once, when I opened a bin to measure out corn, I reached in to grasp hold of what I thought was the measure but unfortunately it turned out to be a rat trap and I suddenly found my fingers in a vice-like grip. It was very painful.

The managers were, Thomas Knowles and Arthur Dodgson, who had earlier served his time as an apprentice there. Other employees were Miss Seed and Edgar Ramskill who worked in the office. Mary worked there during the war.

C Knowles and Sons shop, Main Street, High Bentham in 1904. Christopher Knowles standing in centre. Believed Arthur Tustin's father - Police Sergeant - in foreground with his Ivy Three, belt driven motor cycle. The villagers are awaiting Edward VII (King Teddy) passing through on his way to spend a weekend at Ingleborough Hall to visit the Farrar family (shooting weekend).

Christopher Knowles and Sons shop, Main Street, High Bentham, in 1930's.
Standing in doorway left to right: Miss Seed, Frank Butterfield (Mary Butterfield's father), Rosie
Rosethorn and Herbert Slinger   *Mary Butterfield*

Picture of window display taken on 17th May 1929 in which they won a competition for their display of
Heinz products.   *Mary Butterfield*

Fred Anderson was the traveller taking over from the first Christopher Knowles, who always went on his rounds by pushbike. Coming back in the dark one night, he was robbed by a masked man on Skipton Gate Hill, near Burton-in-Lonsdale. Being a Quaker he decided to take no further action. Bob Foster looked after the horse. Ernie McKay's two daughters from Calf Cop, Rosie Rosethorn from Wennington, Bert Slinger and Frank Butterfield all served in the shop and I delivered the orders.

Christopher Knowles' son Frank, was a staunch Labour Supporter. I remember him standing on the green in Burton-in-Lonsdale, spouting Labour policies around 1926 and nobody taking heed. He was very friendly with Malcolm MacDonald, the son of Ramsey MacDonald, who became Labour Prime Minister, from 1929-35. Once, around this time Ramsay came to give a talk in Bentham Town Hall. He stayed with Frank's sister who lived next door to Vale View, Uncle John's house.

Soon after, Frank met a girl from Lincoln, married her and stood as Parliamentary Candidate for the Isle of Ely but was not successful. So he and his wife went out to Australia, where he worked for the Forestry Commission as a lumberjack. Two daughters were born there, Janie and Dorothy. A few years later when they all returned to England, he brought back with him a certain cactus plant, occasionally burning pieces at home to remind him of the bush in Australia.

Once Frank Butterfield borrowed the firm's vehicle and left it on a hill in gear. It ran backwards into a car. Fortunately, there was not much damage to either vehicle. Edgar Ramskill who later married Mary's sister, Margaret, became manager of the Knowles' shop, in Clapham, where besides groceries and newspapers, over the counter medicines were sold, such as aspirin and cough mixture. Teddy Harrison was the errand boy at that time. My main job besides the other jobs I did, was to make all the deliveries round the villages and up the dales to the outlying farms, some of which were almost inaccessible. It was a long tiring job with the horse and cart, so in 1930, the managers acquired our first motor vehicle. It was a Ford wagon with three gears and solid tyres which had wooden spoked wheels. It was a brute to start with a starting handle, which had a kick like a mule! It was bought from Barton Townley's in Lancaster and the engine was never really in good order. It developed a dreadful noise and had to be taken frequently into Lancaster in order to try and sort out the problem.

I clearly remember when it arrived. There was great excitement in the shop that day. We loaded it up with groceries for the Clapham shop and the man from Barton Townleys, with me sitting beside him, drove it to Clapham and back. He gave me instructions from time to time and when we arrived back in Bentham he just said with no further ado, "You're on your own, now!" I had never driven a vehicle before, so as you can imagine, I was rather nervous at first but soon got the hang of it.

I never took a test. There were no driving tests in 1930, legislation for the Road Traffic Act was passed in 1934 and the first tests took place in 1935, at the cost of 7/6d (37½p) per test. I believe tests were abandoned during the war years but resumed immediately afterwards.

Fred Anderson who was courting a girl from Lancaster at the time owned a car, the first Rover in Bentham. It had a variable gear. He kindly offered to bring me back from Lancaster each time I took the Ford to Barton Townley's. I've never played so much gooseberry in all my life! Sometimes it was well after midnight when I got home and Mary was none too pleased. Fred eventually married the girl. Her name was Violet. Sadly they are both gone.

Barton Townley's finally decided to do a clean swap - the Ford wagon for a Morris Commercial. I was in charge of the wagon and Bob Foster continued to make the horse and cart deliveries to places I couldn't reach with the vehicle. The wagon had a split windscreen and unfortunately after driving up the dales in bitterly cold conditions, by the end of the winter I had developed iritis from the draught. Dr Troughton came and said, "I am going away for a fortnight, so I am going to give you a double dose of eyedrops." He tipped them into my eyes with a teaspoon. My tongue went thick and I couldn't speak. The drops were poisoning me. He immediately sent me to see a specialist in Queen's Square, Lancaster. The fee was two guineas. The older specialist had with him a younger trainee, who insisted that I needed an operation to cure my problem. Thankfully the specialist said, "A month's bed rest, with hot water bottles and hot baths to sweat it out, will do the trick," and it did. He also prescribed mild eye drops. I was off work for six weeks.

Dr Troughton's wife, sadly had been killed in 1912, in probably the first car accident in Bentham. Some horses ran into them, as they were driving home across Newby Moor late one night after visiting a patient. She hit her head on a stone when the car overturned and died a few hours later, from a brain haemorrhage.

By this time Dr Dowell had become our GP. Our only son, John, was born in our attic room, on the 12th May, 1931. I remember dashing down Station Road to the doctor's at 2 am and shouting frantically into a speaking tube, at the door. Dr Leslie Dowell and his wife, Dr Elizabeth, both hurried back with me and John was born very soon afterwards.

He was a healthy little chap and our pride and joy. We came to live downstairs with Mary's mother after John was born. This allowed Mary to put him out in the fresh air and be close at hand. Living with relatives isn't always easy. Mary's mother, Agnes, could be quite a stern task master and kept Mary very busy. Spring cleaning was a much harder job then, than it is today. Everything was turned out of every room. All furniture was washed with vinegar and water, then polished. Carpets were dragged out and beaten on the lawn, curtains washed and left to blow in the breeze. Floor surrounds were waxed and everything had to be back in place by the end of the day. Margaret worked in Lancaster as a telephonist, so was away from it all. Sometimes tensions built up and frustrations crept in but on the whole, we all got along quite well.

Sadly, when I returned to England, one at a time my teeth began to decay, mostly due to the change of food and it wasn't long before I was wearing false teeth. Nowadays, a dentist will do his best to save a tooth but back in those days around 1930, the only remedy for a few bad teeth was to remove the lot.

Squire Taylor at Waterside Pottery, Burton-in-Lonsdale, sitting cross legged weaving baskets of willow for the one and two gallon bottles. *Henry Bateson*

Waterside Pottery by the River Greta around 1900 *Henry Bateson*

The dentist in Bentham in the late 1920's, was a Mr Smith. His practice was in Lancaster but he came over to Bentham once a week, usually on Market Day which was, and still is, on Wednesday. He had rooms in the Main Street and on the morning I went to see him, there was no suggestion of repairing any of the broken teeth. He just said, "I'll take half out this week and the other half next week!" When I came round from the gas, he looked dishevelled and hot and I was lying on the floor with blood all over the place. He said, "You are certainly a rough customer but I'll quieten, you young man!" The following week he gave me a pill before the gas and when I awoke, all was calm. A month later, I was sporting my new teeth.

I was only paid a pound a week for working for C Knowles & Sons but life wasn't dull and I certainly had some interesting times. I remember one morning setting out at 8 o'clock to deliver one ton of provender to a farm up Keasden. The farm was on the top of a steep hill and after reaching the last gate, the path petered out so I left the lorry in the gateway and proceeded the rest of the way on foot, carrying the one hundred weight sacks, one at a time up to the farm. There was no offer of help from the farmer and after about the fifth sack it began to rain. Each sack I heaved on to my back made me wetter and by the time I had been up that hill twenty times I was soaked to the skin. To my horror when I returned to the lorry it had sunk up to the axles in mud. The farmer eventually came down the hill to see what my problem was. He said, "You'll never back out of there! The only way is to roll down this steep field to the gate, then down the next field to the gate at the bottom and out on to the rough track. Then you can back out to the road at the end." So off I went bumping down the first long field, then through the gate and on down another steep gradient to the bottom gate. Then my next problem. The lorry was too wide for the gateway. Wearily I traipsed back up the long hill to ask the farmer for a spade, then down again. Laboriously I dug out a gate stoop and drove out onto the track. I jumped out into the still pouring rain and replaced the stoop trampling in the earth around it as best I could in such soggy conditions. Then up the long haul again to return the spade. Next was the tricky manoeuvre of backing all the way down the long winding track to the road. I arrived home about four in the afternoon instead of ten in the morning and Mary played shell. She had been worried sick as she thought I had had an accident. What a day!

One farm in that area was so spotless you could literally eat off the floor. You can imagine my surprise, however, when on my next visit I found the farm had changed hands and so had the circumstances. Across the flagged kitchen floor, lay a young tree with the end of it burning in the grate. It was gradually pushed along to the fireplace until the whole lot had burnt away.

I used to buy a tree top occasionally from a Mr and Mrs Nelson, who farmed across from the Ridding, just outside Low Bentham and I paid half a crown for the wood. I cut it into logs and borrowed the shop vehicle to transport it to Grassrigg, where I stacked it by the house ready for winter use. Mr Slinger had some hen huts in a nearby field which besides hens housed a number of rats. Some came into the wood pile and when eventually the huts were demolished the resident rats found a broken vent in our house wall and made their way into the attic. Mary was horrified. I bought a substance called 'Liverpool Virus' and put it under the rafters and a bowl of water on the floor. It smelled so delicious I felt I could have eaten it myself. For two days we heard the rats running about up there. Then they were gone probably leaving the same way they had entered. I immediately repaired the ground level vent. We never saw them again!

Annie Robinson who worked in the Clapham Shop was engaged to be married and once when I was making one of my twice weekly deliveries there, she asked if I would give her a lift to Clapham Station. She wanted to go into Lancaster by train to buy her trousseau. It had started to snow when I arrived in Clapham and by the time I had unloaded, four inches of snow had fallen. The Morris Commercial had a gravity feed and always seemed to stop halfway up hills. This meant climbing out, unloading goods and carrying them up through umpteen gates, then returning for the rest. I got soaked to the skin many a time.

On this particular day, I was taking Annie Robinson to catch a train but as we climbed into the cab the snow was falling thick and fast. Halfway to the station there is a cemetery besides a sharp bend in the road. The vehicle went out of control on the ice and snow and we landed on top of the wall, the front end resting on the oil sump, as the vehicle see-sawed back and forth. There was a big drop behind the wall, so we both had to climb out at the passenger side. All that Annie worried about was that she might miss her train. So she waded off through the snow for the last quarter of a mile and just made it in time. Nearby farmers, the Lund brothers from Crinabottom, got a horse rigged up with chains and pulled me off the wall. Miraculously, there was no damage apart from a slight scrape on the underside and I arrived back home in Bentham safely, with no further problems.

On another occasion when I was driving along by the stream, down below the station at Clapham, I drew to a halt when I saw a rabbit and a stoat in the middle of the road. Neither moved. They both stared fixedly at each other, being quite mesmerised and entirely unaware of my presence. I climbed out of the vehicle and walked over towards them. Still, they didn't move. Slowly, I bent and touched the rabbit, giving it a slight push. Suddenly it was very alert and darted into the hedge bottom. The stoat scurried off in the opposite direction. I don't know how long they would have remained like that if I hadn't come along.

The Morris Commercial did so much good work for Knowles shop. The hardest journeys especially in bad weather were the journeys where I had to contend with gated roads, such as Lowgill, Kingsdale Head, Dent and Hawes roads. Many a time I've been soaked to the skin by the time I have arrived back to Bentham.

Arthur Dodgson was the Wesleyan choirmaster and used to organise children's romps to farms. I used to take them in the Morris Commercial which had a canvas top. The journey was always accompanied by giggles and squeals of excitement. It was wonderful to see the pleasure these children had romping about on the hay and climbing in the barns, stroking the kittens, of which there always seemed to be many litters. The picnic teas and the sweets distributed afterwards were always a highlight. By the time they were ready for home with energy spent, a subdued sometimes sleepy group climbed into the back of the vehicle for the journey home. Cowan Bridge was one of the favourite destinations.

On one groceries' delivery I broke down in Dentdale quite near to the viaduct. I was about a mile from the nearest telephone which was at Dent Station. I rang through to Bentham, after crossing rough terrain in the pouring rain and Thomas Knowles said he would pick me up in his American Overland. Whilst I awaited his arrival I rang the garage in Dent. They came out immediately and towed the Commercial into Luffman's farmyard where it would later be repaired. These things always seemed to happen on Saturdays when my work was done for free.

Mr and Mrs Luffman were kindness itself. I knew them because they had previously lived up Keasden and I used the Commercial to move them to their farm near Dent. There was a wonderful avenue of trees up to the farm. It was very picturesque with a splendid tree in the farmyard, with a stream running by. Sometimes Mary would travel with me for the outing and Mrs Luffman always made us welcome with cups of tea and snacks.

Once, I had Mary and John, who was about eighteen months old with me as we travelled home from Dent. We hadn't gone far when suddenly there was a terrific thunderstorm with torrential rain and lightning which seemed never ending. Mary was afraid for our safety but John seemed to enjoy the whole thing. We had to stop on the tops until the worst was over. Thankfully we got home safely.

About the time we bought our Morris Commercial, a local farmer was one of the first people in the area to have a two stroke Rover. He used to come into Bentham to buy sacks of cattle feed and was such an awkward driver that everyone used to come out and watch his antics. The only other vehicle in Bentham at this time, belonged to Pye's, the provender merchants, by the station.

There was an ex-farmer's wife from Keasden called Mrs Taylor. She was a tiny little woman. I remember her getting married one Saturday morning and spending the rest of the day working in the hayfields. After the birth of her first child, she was told by her doctor not to have any more children or she would endanger her life, but amazingly she produced nine more and outlived her husband. After his death and her retirement, she came to live near Clapham Station. She had a back stone made over her fire and she made riddle bread from fine oatmeal. (The back stone is a flat stone that is cemented over the boiler. The flue drew the heat under it and it was slightly greased to bake on). The oatmeal from our shop was rather on the coarse side, so I made a special sieve to refine the oatmeal for her. I left the oatmeal at her house on Tuesday mornings and called back later in the afternoon, when she had a large batch of riddle bread ready for me to bring back to the Bentham shop, to store in the cool cellar. She always had a cup of tea ready for me. On Wednesdays she would get on her push bike, cycle over to Bentham, collect her riddle bread and sell it on the market.

I often brought half a cured pig back from distant farms. We would cut it up for the farmers, or slice it on the bacon slicer and returned it on my next visit up the dales, free of charge.

One farmer's wife where I delivered provisions made excellent use of our cotton meal bags. She used to cut a hole in the bottom, cut off the bottom corners and use them for overalls. Her husband owned a Royal Enfield 1,000 cc V-Twin motorcycle with a box sidecar. He always had to run it down the hill from the farm to get it started. When in Bentham, his son had to race down the street pushing the bike until it started, then leaping into the sidecar at the last minute. Once he leapt but missed the sidecar and his father sailed off without him! He was none too happy about that.

When out on my rounds, I often bought butter, cheese and eggs from some of the farmers and loaded it into the wagon for the return journey. Most of our butter was bought in wooden boxes from the wholesaler because just occasionally the butter from the farms turned rancid. The price of butter and eggs was set in Bentham every Wednesday on market day, butter being usually about fourpence a pound and eggs around a shilling a dozen.

I was travelling along the Wray road one day and turned off towards Lowgill. The farm where I was making deliveries had a very narrow lane down into the farmyard. I opened the gate into the yard and was surprised to see a Pye's provender vehicle upside down in a huge hole, where the yard had collapsed. It lay in a flowing stream of beautiful crystal water. The strange thing was, that up until that time the farmer had no proper water supply for cooling his milk, so had to sell his milk round. What meagre supply he had came from a pipe in the road one eighth of a mile away, which he had paid to be installed, whilst all the time he had this wonderful supply beneath his farmyard!

Apart from five years during the war, I worked for C Knowles & Sons for twelve years and only ever earned, one pound a week. I sometimes asked for a rise but was always put off. I think that for last few months of service my wage went up by half a crown.

I was once travelling towards Burton-in-Lonsdale, when William Woodburn, who worked for the Council organising road cleaning etc, flagged me down and pointed to the sky. I got out of my vehicle and looked in the direction he was pointing and there hovering gracefully in the sky, was a Zeppelin. In the brilliant sunshine, it looked like a huge golden marrow. It was a wonderful sight and well worth stopping to see. It was the only time I saw a dirigible balloon.

Several of the farms where I delivered groceries were almost inaccessible. One such farm belonged to a Mr Price who lived in Keasden. His farm was called 'Hawks Heath' and a stream had to be crossed to reach it. Sometimes the stream was so full that crossing it was impossible. Mr Price built a hut at the bottom of the hill where merchants could leave their wares to be collected by him when the stream subsided. He filled the back of the hut with logs for sale and whenever Bob Foster delivered provisions up there by horse and trap he brought back a load of logs for Arthur Dodgson. The same happened on Saturday mornings after potato deliveries to Ingleton Model Village, which was built initially in the early 1920's, to house the Ingleton coal pit workers. Whoever made the delivery always brought back a load of coal from the pit for Arthur Dodgson. 'Rabbity Dick' lived in Keasden and caught rabbits to sell to anyone who wanted to buy them. He used the hut as a collection point. Christopher Knowles Shop almost went backrupt in the early thirties. Miners living in the Model Village hardly ever paid for goods delivered and often did a 'moonlit flit'!

I remember delivering provender to a house up Back Gate, in Ingleton. The owner had an obsolete earth lavatory behind his house and wanting to put it to good use, decided to put a pig in there. For weeks I delivered meal and watched the pig grow rapidly.

Soon it was enormous and the owner suddenly realized that the pig was far too large to come through the door.

The last time I saw it, a group had gathered and a long discussion was taking place with suggestions as to how to extract the pig from the building. I'm afraid I didn't stay around to watch and since no further deliveries were required I never did discover how they solved their problem!

Another farm up at Dent Head where I delivered groceries and provender was called 'The Cobbles' and was owned by a Mr and Mrs Greenbanks. This was one of the more inaccessible places and the Greenbanks also had a hut built at the foot of the rough track. It was a great help to people making deliveries.

At one farm below Dent Head there was no proper track. In winter, when the ground was hard, I had to run round the field to catch a horse which would then be tethered to the waiting sledge. The provisions would be packed on and away we would go to the top of the hill. It was warm work, I can tell you!

Situated at the top of the open moorland above Clapham was 'The Kennels'. It belonged to the Farrar Estate at Clapham. The dogs used for fox hunting and grouse shooting on the moors were looked after there by the gamekeeper. I delivered the dog food.

The Duke of Westminter's land which ranged between Slaidburn, Dent and Lancaster, joined the Farrar estate and the Duke sometimes came over for the shooting. His land covered thirty-six thousand acres.

King Edward VII often came for weekends to 'Ingleborough Hall' to visit the Farrar family. He came especially for the shooting. We sometimes saw him striding across the Station Yard, at Clapham. He was quite a small man.

I believe, Dr Farrar sometimes rented out his land to a French firm during the hunting season.

I have some fond memories of the early horse fairs, hiring days, show days, fun fairs and auctions at Bentham. The horse fairs were held once a year in June. Travellers on their way to Appleby Fair would arrive in Bentham the eve before trading day. The actual day was always busy and exciting as the dealers ran their horses up and down the streets. The horses were mostly for riding or for light traps and were always in excellent condition. There were no shire horses. Trade was done mainly between the farming community and people owning private traps or carriages.

If the day had been successful then evening found the four public houses

A Zeppelin, pictured above the Police House, in Main Street, High Bentham in the 1920's. Leslie Reid's shop on the right of the picture was burnt to the ground during February 1953.

Bernard Williams

Haymaking on Mrs Harrisons farm, Calf Cop, Low Bentham around the early 1900's - reminds me of the early Hiring Days!

Miss E Willan   (David Johnson Collection)

crowded out. There was a lot of drinking and many fights broke out but on the whole it was a good day. The following morning all was neatly packed into caravans and the travellers continued their journey to Appleby, tethering their horses on many grass verges along the way. Their favourite places for overnight stops in our area were Melling Moor, Kirkby Lonsdale, Middleton, Sedbergh and of course Bentham. In later years as motor traffic increased, the local horse fairs and hiring days petered out.

Hiring always took place between the 21st and 22nd of June. Many men came over from Ireland by boat to Heysham and then by train to Bentham, where they crowded at 'The Cross' which is the junction, between 'The Brown Cow' (now the Coach House'), 'The Black Bull' and Christopher Knowles' Shop. Others gathered in front of 'The Royal Oak Hotel'.

Each man was offered a shilling by the farmer who wanted to hire him and told what duties he would be expected to perform. If he accepted the shilling then this was regarded as a binding hiring agreement for one month. There was very little machinery in those days so lots of manpower was needed on the busy farms. The men were hired mostly for haytime but if it rained they were expected to clean horse trappings, clean out and whitewash cow sheds and even do muck-spreading.

If the farmer had hired more than one man, then at haytime, the men cut by working in rows. The grass was then stooked to dry, later to be stacked or carted into barns. The men brought their own scythes with them.

Haytime was hard but had its rewards. There were refreshing drinks and picnic baskets brimming with tasty snacks brought out to the fields when the worker would rest awhile, amidst the glorious aroma of new mown hay and the song of overhead skylarks. These were most refreshing breaks from their labours.

Sometimes one month was not long enough to complete the set tasks and then the farmer would offer a further month's work at the same rate of pay, with a new binding agreement made. But after the first month, most of the men were anxious to return to their families, in Ireland.

During their time in England some of the men had to sleep rough either in barns or sheds. One farmer, that I know of, would not even allow his hired men to eat at the same table as himself and his family but the majority treated their men well.

Dan O'Neil came over from Ireland around 1929, for the Hiring. One afternoon he sat on School Hill watching the children play. He was so impressed by their well turned out appearance, that he decided there and then, to remain in Bentham, where he lived out his life. He found work farming and then worked for the Council, finally marrying a Magoolagan girl. They had five children, Mary, Margaret, Catherine, Bernard and Peter. Sadly Peter, was tragically killed at a young age whilst working for the Council.

Another man who came over from Ireland in the 1920's, was Ernie McKay. He was a cattle dealer and brought stock over by boat to Heysham. The animals were then driven on foot to Low Bentham where he lived in a cottage at Calf Cop. He had a few acres of land there. Along the way he would call in on many of his farmer friends often selling off some of his cattle. Sometimes he would arrive home with very few left. These would be sold at auction on Wednesdays. Hens were also brought in crates from Ireland, all to be sold at auction.

In the 1930's, Bentham on market day was always full of noise and bustle, with horse drawn vehicles in the streets, such as brewery drays, farm carts, coal and fruit carts, as well as private traps. Anyone with a bucket and shovel could collect plenty of nourishment for their rhubarb and roses. People milled around the many stalls. The farming community made good use of Wednesdays, selling a large variety of dairy products, home-made cakes, biscuits, fruit, vegetables, preserves, plants, flowers, baskets, brooms and other household products. It was quite a familiar sight to see a farmer and his lad, with a dog, meandering through the streets, driving their herds of cattle and flocks of sheep to auction.

Of course, nowadays things are much more civilised at the mart. The animals arrive in wagons or trucks and there are many good places to park. The mart also has its own cafe, 'The Byres', where the farming community, in fact anyone, can obtain a substantial meal for a very reasonable price.

I remember one morning, there was something of a commotion outside the auction mart. A cow had gone missing. You can imagine the hilarity it caused, when the animal was discovered up in the bathroom of Mrs Parrington's cottage next to the mart. It was much better than television watching the antics of the two young lads who were trying to extract the cow from that small bathroom. First, they had to turn the creature round, which was no mean feat in such a confined space. Then there was the matter of getting it to descend to ground level. After much pushing, prodding and coaxing, the task was achieved. To the great relief of the lads and the owner of the cottage, the cow emerged amid cheers and laughter from the many onlookers!

Mrs Parrington must have been greatly relieved when the cow was finally ousted. Her son had a shoe shop in Bentham quite near to the auction mart. He was a quiet, rather religious man and a local preacher. Often he could be seen reading his Bible as he walked along the edge of the pavement and sometimes in the gutter on his way to Chapel.

Another incident concerned a man called Teddy, who lived on his own, in a small cottage going out towards Clapham. One market day he came down into Bentham and called at Joe Winn's Hardware Shop. Frank Butterfield was serving and Teddy said to him, "I've got a terrible smell in my cottage and I can't get rid of it!" Frank said, "Perhaps it's coming from under the skirting! I suggest you take this tin of creosote and paint round the edges of your flagged floor, at least it will smell nicer!"

Teddy went home and duly painted round his floor until he came to the hearth, which had a York fireplace with a boiler for hot water on one side and an oven, which Teddy hardly ever used on the other. I know he thought, "I'll pour some of this creosote into the oven. The warmth will permeate the smell all over the house." You can imagine his horror when he opened the oven door only to find

Wednesday Market Day in High Bentham - 1930's
A familiar sight in those days - cattle being driven through the village to market

Mrs Jennie Cardus

Wednesday Market Day in High Bentham - 1930's. Stall holders - country people meeting to bring and buy and meet up to talk

High Bentham County Primary School Collection

a dead decomposing cat reclining on the oven shelf!

The next amusing tale was told to me by Mary. She was in the hairdresser's one market day, when a very red-faced customer came in saying that she had just had the most embarrassing moment of her life! Being market day, she thought that she would look in at the auction mart. On seeing her friend on the other side of the ring, she gave her a friendly wave, only to discover a few minutes later that she had bought half a dozen calves. She was extremely ashamed and apologetic as she explained to an angry auctioneer, that she couldn't possibly keep the animals because she only lived in a council house.

Coal, coke and other loose commodities arrived in Bentham by train. There was a public weighbridge, behind the Station and the porter was in charge of it. I can't bring to mind the fees, probably because I didn't deal with that side of things. A monthly account was sent to C Knowles & Sons. When I went to collect coal etc, my lorry was weighed before and after loading. Bagged goods, such as flour, sugar, potatoes, provender and many others, did not need to be weighed. There was a Toll Bar just outside Low Bentham and to save many miles of travel when delivering goods to customers just the other side, I had to pay a toll of 2/6d (12 ½p) each way.

Horses brought loads of pots, over from the Potteries, at Burton-in-Lonsdale, to be dispatched by train. The carts never returned empty but were filled with coal which of course had to be weighed, on the weighbridge. Kilns take tons of coal to light. It was thirsty work for the horses, the roads between Burton and Bentham being quite hilly and there used to be a large stone water trough near the railway bridge, where the animals could drink their fill before the return journey.

Bentham Agricultural Show was always an important event and still is. The shows I remember were always a hive of industry, with horse jumping, classes for farm animals, domestic animals, cage birds and hens. There were lots of competitions in many different tents, for cut flowers, house plants, fruit and vegetables, and in more modern times, flower arranging, arts and craft, needlework, wine making, photography, and a domestic tent for all the wonderful bread, cakes and other delicacies.

In those days, the event was held in a field down Station Road, on the other side of the railway bridge beside the River Wenning. There was a refreshments' tent, where the local ladies provided tea, sandwiches and delicious home-made cakes.

The children always enjoyed Show Day. There were egg and spoon, three-legged and sack races. There were even races and tug-o-war for the adults. Sometimes steam or traction engines would gather in one corner of the field or the latest motor car or motor cycle would be displayed. Occasionally it rained and then the field became a quagmire, with all the farm traffic and hundreds of feet trampling the ankle deep mud but nobody seemed to mind! The tent interiors had a smell of their own, a smell I would know anywhere. It was a cross between the stronger smelling vegetables, fruit and the heavy scent of flowers and moist grass crushed beneath feet. It was quite unmistakable.

There was always plenty of drink around and I remember one stall holder who had taken a few over the odds, calling out from his fruit cart, "Pears a pound - plums same!" He never gave us a price.

As the afternoon came to a close, people began to disperse and trundle their way back up Station Road for a couple of hours rest before the Fun Fair in the evening. This was usually held in the field behind Goodenber Road. There were dodgem cars, roundabouts, swing boats, a small ferris wheel, hoopla stalls, coconut shies, a rifle range and other fair games. Sometimes there would be a gypsy to tell fortunes.

In the Town Hall a dance would be in full swing in the large upstairs room. Everyone would be wearing their best bib and tucker as they danced the night away to the strains of Newbolds or Cathy Parker's band, or the beautiful playing of Fred Cook at the piano. At midnight everyone went home. A wonderful time was had by all and show day was over for another year!

We had three pet dogs, one after the other and they were all called, 'Tinker', we just liked the name! The first was a black and tan Alsatian. We were very proud of it and entered it in Bell Busk Show. It was highly commended. The sad part was that when we let it out into the garden at Grassrigg we caught children tormenting it with sticks through the gate and it became rather temperamental. When it was twelve months old one of Mary's aunts came to visit and sat in Tinker's favourite chair. It bit her and sadly had to be put down.

Our second 'Tinker' came to us unexpectedly. Mary's brother, George, had seen an advert in the paper for the sale of St Bernard puppies. George fancied owning one and sent off his order and money by post. He got a letter saying the dog would arrive by train at Bentham Station and when the time came for its arrival, he hurried excitedly down to collect it. You can imagine his embarrassment when his St Bernard turned out to be a little brown and white mongrel! He was so ashamed at having been duped that he hid it in his coat and brought it up to us. "You can keep it!" he said and made a quick exit. He turned out to be a most delightful little creature of great character. He had a glossy coat and a beautiful bushy tail, nearly everybody in Bentham got to know him. He was friendly and went visiting every house down the street each day. He would often travel down to Low Bentham on the bus by himself and return the same way. All the bus drivers knew him. His favourite pastimes were to precede the silver bands down the street at band contests and follow all funerals. Auctions at Turners were a must and Bring and Buy Sales he found very exciting. Public Meetings were attended frequently. No one minded him sitting in at the back, which he did silently wagging his tail from time to time. The only meetings from which he was sometimes turned away were Council Meetings in the Town Hall. They probably didn't want him to know their business! He also inspected all events at the Bentham Agricultural Shows. When we took him for a walk he would wait until we were almost home then silently disappear, reappearing about midnight barking at the door to be let in. He died about a year after John was born.

Our third 'Tinker' was a thoroughbred brown Spaniel from Newby. He was a bit wayward, so we sent him up to a farm near the Big Stone, above Bentham, to

Mrs Ann Smith and her daughter-in-law Mrs Daisy Smith early 1920's at Low Bentham Toll Bar. Charges started at a penny each way for bicycles to a shilling for horse drawn wagons or vans. People were charged double between the hours of 10pm and 6am The road was open to the public on 3 May 1932   *Miss E Willan (David Johnson Collection)*

THE BIG STONE, BENTHAM.

Jane Preston

Big Stone, above Bentham - a popular attraction. People gathered here celebrating Jubilee year in 1897 be trained. The man was called Mr Dunn and he couldn't do anything with him, so sent him back to us.

When I was away during the war years I wrote to Mary almost every day. Tinker would sort out my letter from the rest of the post and take it up to Mary in our bedroom. He developed a liver problem and when the vet saw him, he said the kindest thing would be to put him to sleep. Sadly he died at the age of thirteen just before I was demobbed. John who was then about fifteen and his Uncle Edgar (Margaret's husband), buried him beneath the cherry tree at Grassrigg. We had no more dogs after that.

We made our own amusements in those days. We had many happy musical evenings in our home. The Butterfield boys would come and Norman would play his trumpet. Edwin Jackman played his violin, whilst Jack Leaming, Mary Leaming and I sang. My Mary accompanied us on the piano. We always ended these evenings with games and once when playing musical chairs, a rather hefty lady, flung herself on to our brand new settee and broke all the springs!

Mary and I both sang in the Bentham Choral Society, which was conducted by the Headmaster of Bentham School. I sang tenor and Mary soprano. We also went to Choral Concerts and plays in the Town Hall. I remember Wilcock Whittaker directing 'The Lady's not for Burning' by Christopher Fry. It was very well performed by the Phoenix Players. Little did I know that I would meet the author in my army days.

Bentham Silver Band in the 1950's marching through the street at Town End, Bentham at the head of a procession. Tinker used to love following them!   *Mr James Robinson*

I was a keen gardener, I used to grow tobacco amongst other things and cured it in the attic we had vacated after John's birth. I would string the leaves across the room until they were dry, then coated them with a mixture of honey, water, salt petre and rum. It was then laid flat in a wooden press. It smelled wonderful when it was rolled up to mature. I smoked some of the tobacco myself and the rest I gave to Frank Fisher and to my first Librarian, who smoked it in his pipe. He said it was the best tobacco he had ever smoked!

I often played tennis on the courts where there is now a bowling green. All in all we were never short of pleasant things to do.

We attended Meeting every Sunday morning at the Friends Meeting House, in Main Street, Bentham. In the afternoons we walked across the fields to Calf Cop, at Low Bentham for afternoon Meeting.

The early thirties were very hard times and those in any kind of employment were most fortunate. In 1936 during the depression, a protest march was made by two hundred unemployed shipbuilders from Jarrow, near Newcastle-upon-Tyne, to London. We were led to believe that money was so tight. Yet when war broke out there was ample money for armaments and good wages for all the newly employed who made them.

Chapter Seven
THE WAR YEARS

On 3rd September, 1939 war was declared with Germany. After taking a first aid course, I volunteered for the Friends Ambulance Corps but was not accepted, so I became a Special Constable. I remember I had to tell a certain lady in Bentham that a chink of light was showing between her blackout curtains. She was so annoyed that she never spoke to me again!

Not only did house windows have to be darkened, but street lights were disconnected, car headlights had shields with slots so that the light from them was directed downwards and buses crept along, virtually in the dark. All signposts were removed and iron railings compulsorily taken away for scrap.

During the early part of the war a man called Fred Hellowell, being of the Quaker faith, refused to fight and with the help of the Friends Relief Service, set up 'The Stone Bower Fellowship' at Burton-in-Lonsdale in 1940. It was originally for homeless people from Liverpool. Although many local people criticized him for being what they called, 'a conscientious objector', they soon became aware of the good work he was doing. He sometimes had as many as thirty residents and then it became necessary to move to larger premises. 'The Stone Bower Fellowship' moved to the Cove, at Silverdale. Fred sadly died on 11th May 1984 but his good work continued and in 1995, the Cove became an Abbeyfield Home.

In 1940 I was still delivering groceries. Feizor was one of my favourite places for deliveries. It was so pretty. I used to come out near the top of Buckhaw Brow and buy petrol from the garage there. It was two shillings and four pence per gallon and I used to bring back twenty, two gallon tins to Bentham. Soon after this, petrol was rationed.

Buckhaw Brow, near Settle, was very steep until the early sixties, when some of the steepness was slightly levelled. Until then lorries travelling up the brow climbed at about five miles per hour. Youngsters would hide on the roadside and as the lorries crawled slowly up the hill they would dart out, clamber onto the lorries and steal whatever they could lay their hands on, hence the saying, "It fell off the back of a lorry!" I believe there were several court cases about this thieving.

In the early years of the war I was once travelling from Clapham Station to Eldroth, when a German plane flew alongside me following the railway line. It was so close that I could see the airmen walking up and down inside the plane. They were obviously on reconnaissance. Two nights later there was a bombing at a farm in Eldroth which had obviously been mistaken for the junction at Clapham Station. The farmer had just had new white asbestos buildings erected and this is why their mistake occurred. Five bombs were dropped on the way up and four more on the way back. Fortunately the farmhouse was not damaged apart from the smashed windows and nobody was hurt but the residents were obviously left in shock. People came from miles to see the damage.

About 1943 a German Messerschmitt plane was placed almost opposite

Grassrigg up Goodenber Road, Bentham. A fee of sixpence was charged to sit in it and the money went towards the war effort. I remember, the metal having a peculiar smell. Some children, including John scrambled over it and in it without paying. It remained in Bentham for only a short time, perhaps two or three weeks when it would then be removed for display in other villages around the country.

At Grassrigg during the war we had two Jewish refugees staying with us, one from Poland and one from Austria. They had briefly been interned in Peel Castle on the Isle of Man. The Austrian was called Ernest and worked for a while at Butts Farm. Later he worked for the Government and then went out to Africa to instruct in manual skills, agriculture and well digging. He came to England to see us from time to time and on his return to Africa he always took back a new Land Rover. The Polish man went into the Forces and became a pilot. He left his precious expensive Leica camera with us for safe keeping and returned for it at the end of the war.

I joined the Forces in 1941. I was called before a Tribunal at the Corn Exchange in Preston. Since my marriage I had become a Quaker but had been attending Meetings since my return from Australia. The Tribunal consisted of four pompous men. Because of my age (37), I was to join the Non-Compatant Corps (NCC) but when I said I could not bring myself to take human life, they asked me if I had ever used a rifle. I had to confess that I had often used a rifle in Australia to kill animals for food. They decided to put me in the Pioneer Corps, No 6 Company and sent me off to Huyton, near Liverpool, for six weeks training. Our Companies ranged from 1-6. I remember Christopher Fry, the writer, being in No 1 Company.

Huyton was a suburb and the houses we bunked in were just in the process of being built. There were no doors and we had to sleep on palliasses (thin straw mattresses) on the floors. Straw for them was collected from nearby farms and was often wet. Men began to go downhill fast because they were never dry.

After training we went to Blundell Sands. We were billeted in a rather posh area in Stanley House, a large seafront gentleman's residence. We still slept on palliasses with one blanket and an overcoat. We slept on the floor in a ring with our feet in the middle. While we were there we went fire watching every night on the docks at Bootle. There were large mills and warehouses along the waterfront and these we patrolled. This went on for about twelve months. We snatched an odd half hour of sleep when we could. Most of us were sent up to guard the top of these buildings and during air raids there was absolutely no shelter as the place was open to the heavens.

We had a not very nice Sergeant whom I thought was far too strict and unkind. He always managed to stay well below in places of safety during raids. Some of the lads decided to get their own back on him by dropping debris from the fourth floor purposely missing him, but nevertheless, giving him a dreadful fright. He seemed to ease up on us after that but not when it came to the gruelling marches he put us through during the day. They just about killed some of the men.

On nights, once in a while, we were picked to patrol at ground level but always

About 1943 - the German Messerschmitt, which was situated for a fortnight, opposite Grassrigg, Goodenber Road, High Bentham.
Picture taken by Tom Guy of his father Robert Guy standing on far right, sitting in the cockpit is Mr Foster from the Electric Shop and Mrs Nowel holding a basket.

Tom Guy

in twos because of the high crime rate. The two chosen counted themselves most fortunate. There was a bakery close by and whenever possible, the two on duty would stand over the grating beside the bakery, for the benefit of the wonderful warmth permeating upwards and the appetising smell of baking. It was most welcome on wet or freezing winter nights.

A member of the Slinger family from Bentham who used to work for Christopher Knowles, did his training at Blundell Sands and had a distant relative who resided there. He asked me to call on this relative, Mr Warburton. He and his wife made me very welcome and invited Mary and John, who was eleven, to stay. I, of course stayed at Stanley House. Mary came a second time but John was then at Wennington School, which had moved to Wetherby (this was a private Quaker School), so he was never back at Blundell Sands.

I recall one incident which happened whilst at Blundell Sands. A narrow area had been fenced off for access to the bathing beach. The rest of the beach had been laid with mines against enemy invasion. One day a group of young children squeezed through the wire and were found playing in the mined area. Instructions were yelled to them, "Keep perfectly still - stay exactly where you are!" A man from our Company volunteered to try and bring them to safety, which thankfully he managed to do. He was awarded a medal for his bravery but refused to collect it, saying he didn't believe in war.

We were at Blundell Sands for about twelve months, during which time there was constant bombing of the waterfront for about eight weeks when many churches were also destroyed. After those eight weeks all bombing of the area stopped. It seemed strange that the Liver Buildings were never damaged.

Our next move was to Buxton to a place called, 'Dove Holes', one of the highest places in Britain. We worked in huge quarries for a firm called, Taylor Friths. There were two tiers both a quarter of a mile long. These were like giant steps into the hillside, one above the other, so that both could be worked at the same time. Our job was to break down the rocks after they had been blasted from the quarry face. We were each supplied with a seven pound and a two pound hammer in order to break the stone into pieces, no larger than about six inch squares. This was to enable them to pass through the crusher.

A special team of men dealt with the explosives and pill boxes were placed strategically to shelter the men from falling debris. A loud warning whistle was blown before detonation, giving men time to take cover.

The quarry had a special Ford machine which took explosives to where the civilians worked. It had a trailer and I was later given the job of driving it up and down to the quarry face. One day it broke down and a civilian mechanic and myself worked on the engine to get it going again. He was a good living Christian and he taught me a great deal but some of the other civilians were quite unpleasant.

One day I was crossing one of the rail tracks with an empty trailer to collect explosives when the vehicle broke down on the crossing. The men above sent down some loose empty trucks and I just managed to leap to safety before the collision. Fortunately my trailer was not too badly damaged and one of the loose trucks was derailed.

Another job we were required to do was to feed the kilns with coal and limestone. When once the kiln was fired it was seldom allowed to die out because lighting it was such a big job. The coal was shovelled in at the top and when it was well alight the limestone went in on top. As the whole lot burnt the limestone broke up and with the coal and cinders, fell through a grid onto the floor below. This process produced cob lime which had to be sorted by hand from the cinders and lime dust. The lime dust was heaped outside and the cob lime loaded into trucks for the journey to chemical works, where some was added to flour and even toothpaste. Builders used the lime cobs and water added to them, produced quick lime. They used lime, sand and horse hair for plastering walls. Working on the kiln was a filthy job. We all wore handkerchiefs over our noses and mouths for protection against dust and fumes.

The civilian mechanic told me about the former owner of the quarry in the early days, when all that was produced was lime for the land or for paint. He lived twenty miles away, near Manchester and had his own personal train, to bring him into his office each day. The best stone was taken away for lime by canal to Manchester. The rubbish was stacked up in mountainous heaps around the quarry and during the war farmers paid a good price for loads of it to spread on their land. The owner made quite a profit.

A train came every day to Dove Holes with oil and petrol. One of the quarries was sealed so that it could be stored there. A fighter plane patrolled all day but not on foggy days and there were plenty of those.

We walked a mile to the quarry, very early, each cold winter's morning and were always given sandwiches and cocoa for lunch. I got so that I hated even the smell of cocoa. We marched back to camp just after four in the afternoon to a meal followed by evening chores, which consisted of sentry duty, or preparing vegetables for three hundred men in readiness for the next day's evening meal.

We were nearly always tired during our stay at Dove Holes because we had very little sleep, due to the fact that a series of tunnels, ran beneath our billet and night trains hurtling through them kept us all awake. We were billeted in Nissen huts and slept covered with one blanket and overcoat. It being winter time we sometimes awoke to find ourselves covered with ice and condensation. I think we were at Dove Holes for about a year.

Next, we went to Derby. As we marched out of the Station I remember passing the statue of Florence Nightingale which stood outside the hospital there. We were billeted at Alverston, which was a small suburb of Derby. There was just an odd house or two there at the time.

The Government had bought a boggy field there. It was so close to the river that it was often waterlogged. We were frequently up to our knees in mud and were not supplied with wellingtons.

We slept in Nissen huts and our job was to build decent huts with telephones

Army days - This was No 6 Company of the Pioneer Corps (NCC), taken when we were training at Blundell Sands, with Stanley House in the background, in 1941. Jim is sitting down and is centre front.

for the American troops, who were arriving in England. I and many of the other men became ill with rheumatic complaints. It was a fortnight before I was fit to work again. To add insult to injury, the Rolls Royce factory was just up the road making aeroplane engines and when the wind was in a certain direction the noise from there was deafening. Some of the men were driven to distraction.

In one corner of the quagmire were stacked brand new wagons. They were Morris and Fords chiefly but there were also military vehicles. Some were beginning to rust and everything was so overgrown, that they were hardly visible. We passed them everytime we went into town. It was a great waste in such a time of shortage. The Government should never have bought such land. Everytime holes or trenches were dug, they immediately filled with water, which seeped through from the nearby river.

When I went to town to Meeting on Sundays I used to carry my clean shoes under my arm and leave my dirty shoes in the guard room until my return. We spent six months in these filthy conditions.

Our next place of work was a little scattered area called Melbourne, in Derbyshire. We were billeted a couple of miles from our work, in a gentleman's residence which was partly derelict and mostly boarded up. It was guarded at night to protect a beautiful fireplace which had been designed by Christopher Wren. Other nicer parts of the house were also boarded up for protection against damage.

Every day we walked into Melbourne to a Railway Depot. The nearby railway was being extended and train loads of sleepers were arriving from all over the country. It was our job to stack them like pyramids. We weren't there for more than three weeks but it was jolly hard work. Two men carried each sleeper to the pile, then returned to repeat the job all day long. It was back-breaking. We were glad to leave.

I do remember having my first sight of walnut and almond trees full of their autumn fruits. It was great to see but we weren't allowed to pick any.

Next, through Manchester remaining briefly in barracks for a few days and then on to Nottingham, where we worked with the Royal Army Engineers, sorting mail for the Forces. Sorting was done at the Vyella Factory and Christmas arrived at the time I was there. Parcels came from all over the country to be sorted before being sent abroad for the troops. These parcels were piled high in the warehouses. We all had to work around the clock in order to get them away on time. General Montgomery had stacks of tobacco sent from wellwishers. Mail was also collected by wagon from the station and after sorting was returned there.

A certain amount of thieving went on, sometimes dropped into legs of baggy overalls and sometimes passed out through lavatory windows, until the culprits were caught and sentenced to three years' imprisonment, in Nottingham Castle. Was it worth it? We passed the castle on the way back to our billets and often saw the prisoners waving their arms through the barred windows.

One thing we were never short of whilst working at the Vyella Factory was buttons. We used to find them littered everywhere.

Our billet was at the top of a very steep hill going out of Nottingham. Troops would jump onto trolley buses as they slowed to climb the hill and jump off at the top. We were never charged for these short rides.

We were billeted in empty shops. I was on the top floor with one narrow window for fresh air. In the bottom part of the shop was a club for the Irish community. Lots of drink was consumed there and as the evenings progressed it often became very rowdy with fights breaking out. One man was killed whilst we were there. I took part in an identity parade to try and find the culprit. He was not in my line up and I don't know if he was ever found. Part of our stay in Nottingham found us housed in a partly derelict infants' school. It was cold and damp but there was a humourous side to things. The toilets were very tiny and it was hilarious to see a row of grown men seated on these small thrones, which we nicknamed, 'The Rogues Gallery'!

One poor man who was a member of the Plymouth Brethren was taken short just before parade causing him to arrive a few minutes late. Although he explained that the call of nature had to be obeyed, he was nevertheless, put on jankers for a week. Jankers was restrictive punishment, such as potato peeling in the cookhouse or confined to camp.

During our time in Nottingham the army did smoke screening. Little fires made of wood soaked in sump oil were lit all over the city to camouflage the two large railway stations against enemy aircraft attack. These fires produced thick black smoke which discoloured buildings and soiled our clothes and bodies. Many of us contracted dermatitis and had to spend time in hospital. Treatment consisted of being lathered up with a thick white paste and remaining naked for two days, the paste being allowed to dry naturally on the skin. Nostrils and ears were also affected. After two days the infection disappeared. We bathed and dressed completely cured but we remained in hospital a couple of extra days just to make sure.

I came out of my billet one lunch time to return to the Vyella Factory only to bump into a fellow Bentham man called Bert Hemmings. I could hardly believe my eyes. He used to own a garage at the bottom of Goodenber Road and often repaired vehicles for Christopher Knowles. Sometimes he invited me to help in order to cut costs of repairs. I remember he had very high blood pressure and had to have cold baths twice a day. Apparently he was working at a garage just across the road from where I was billeted and he also couldn't believe his eyes at seeing a known friend from Bentham.

Bert kept a Rolls Royce, the first in Bentham. He used it for funerals and marriages and sometimes at weekends he asked me to drive for these occasions. The early Rolls Royce had a sealed engine so if anything went wrong, a trained mechanic had to come out from the factory. Bert and I were good friends. He had two sons, one of whom was killed in the early part of the war.

The wounded were brought from France by trains used as ambulances. As they were unloaded onto the platforms at Nottingham, the stains and the strong smell of blood brought back the dreadful memories of my dear murdered mother. The sight of these poor young men, together with my childhood memories was very upsetting. These same trains were then loaded with mail for the fighting forces.

Lunch times brought sandwiches and cocoa once again. Just across from the station was an ice rink and during the lunch break we were allowed to watch the skaters as a source of relaxation.

Leave was cut to a minimum so Mary visited me and stayed with a Quaker family called McPherson. I, of course, stayed in camp. They were extremely kind and Mary thoroughly enjoyed her visit. John was still at Ingmanthorpe Hall School, Wetherby, so did not go. (Before Wennington Hall School bought the Hall, it had belonged to a wealthy family of Jewellers - Fattorini).

Jack McPherson, his wife and family lived near Nottingham in a classy area called Westbridgeford. Jack started out making badges for blazers and had a special machine to turn them out. He started employing people and his office was at the top of his works and looked out on to the Trent Bridge Cricket and Football Grounds. Jack became the main director of the Trent Bridge Football Club. He expanded his business to make stockings and then in a matter of a few years, his factories sprang up all over the world. He became a millionaire and set all his family up in wealthy businesses. He offered to set Mary and I up in a good grocery business in Nottingham and said he would back us up all the way and we would never go short, but Mary refused the offer, not wanting to be uprooted from our family and friends in Bentham.

He drove a wonderful car called a Sapphire and once took me out in it to his golf club, not to play golf of course, just to watch. The club had a most marvellous view. You could see the countryside rolling into the far distance for miles. Jack's wife was also a member of the club and an excellent golfer. Our company remained in the area for about eighteen months and then we were moved briefly to a place just outside Grantham. It was my job to drive into Grantham for supplies for the airforce and for our barracks. I would drop off the airforce supplies then bring back the remains to camp, which was about ten miles from Grantham. Whilst in this area, I took Mary into Nottingham one evening to see the film, 'Gone with the Wind'. It was a real treat!

Lancaster Castle was our next port of call. It was the time of 'D' Day, which was the 6th June, 1944. We spent most of our time peeling potatoes for between three to four hundred men. This tedious job was carried out on the steps where executions used to take place.

We were billeted in the castle with four men to a cell. The cells were dark, having only one tiny window and were wedge shaped. The walls were about three feet thick. Each cell contained four bunks, one on top of the other. We used to draw straws for the bunks and the one who drew the shortest had to climb up on top.

In between our culinary duties our company was marched down to the Williamson Linoleum and Paint Factory, where we unloaded large wooden boxes which came in by train. They contained mostly dried fruit, dry foods, tobacco, clothing and other commodities. The contents were then repacked in smaller, watertight wooden boxes, to be sent off to the troops in Burma. The Japanese at this time were trying to cut them off from India, a country they (the Japanese) hoped to take over. The boxes were floated secretly down the River Barmaautra to reach the British troops safely without Japanese interference. We also sent huge boxes of quick lime in which to bury their dead.

Although Williamson had done quite a lot of good in Lancaster, amongst other things creating the Williamson Park and monument, he was disliked by the workers who were kept on very low wages.

Mary had told me that during the First World War, in October 1917, there was a massive explosion at the White Lund Armaments Factory, between Lancaster and Morecambe. The noise was so terrific that it could be heard over a thirty miles radius and the fire lasted for three days. The surrounding population didn't know what was going on and many took to the hills thinking that the Germans were attacking. Others hid under viaducts and bridges. In Bentham, Christopher Knowles having a large cellar under his shop allowed as many as wanted to take shelter there. In earlier days the shop had been the Kings Arms Hotel and I believe George Fox was held there for a time on his journey from Lancaster Prison to the east coast. The Knowles family had been in business in Bentham from 1853 and traded from the Kings Arms in 1866, renting it from a Mr Rice who owned the premises and wished to reduce the number of drinking establishments in the town.

The White Lund Armaments or Filling Factory as it was known covered many acres and there were many buildings. Seven thousand women worked there but as it was lunch break, most were outside the buildings and as the explosions started ran to the outside walls. Miraculously on that day only ten people lost their lives and they were mostly fire and maintenance men.

There were many acts of bravery especially on that first day. One in particular was that of an engine driver who dared to go into the blazing exploding buildings and drive a train load of live shells out to safety. There were no further attempts to enter the buildings and after three days of continuous explosions there followed a second large blast resulting in several further fatalities. Today the White Lund Trading Estate now covers most of the blast area.

Although our losses were great during the Second World War it was stated that Russia lost over twelve million people and in support of this statement, someone billeted in the castle, scaled the outside walls after dark and hung a red garment beneath the Union Jack on the flagpole. The next day you can imagine everyone's surprise at seeing this strange red flag fluttering in the morning breeze. We were immediately paraded in the quadrangle and the culprit asked to own up. No one ever did and the offending garment was quickly removed.

Amongst our other duties we sometimes worked in the cookhouse and if our chores were finished by two o'clock, I used to cycle like the wind over to Bentham to spend a few brief hours with my family. This precious time was very quickly over and I cycled back to Lancaster on John's bike, which I was allowed to keep in the guard room. I had to be back in the castle by ten at night.

The eight months stay in Lancaster brought us to the spring of 1945 and our

The White Lund Armaments Factory, Nr Lancaster during the First World War.

move to Hereford where we were stationed near to the auction mart. We were not long in Hereford and we spent much of the time working in the hop fields. Many civilians worked with us and found they could earn a reasonable wage. It had been a very frosty spring and once when returning with supplies to camp my lorry got onto shot ice and went out of control. Luckily no damage was done.

One vivid memory which sticks in my mind was returning to Hereford from leave with a train full of soldiers. When the train stopped outside the station for signals, to my surprise the majority of troops left the train on the wrong side because they didn't have tickets. Only a very few of us remained to alight on the platform.

Victory over Europe came on 8th May, 1945 and there was great rejoicing everywhere. Bells were rung in every church and services of thanksgiving were held. Bonfires were lit up and down the country and lights were switched on in every town and city. It was a glorious sight, after so many years of blackout.

Next came V J Day, on 15th August 1945. We were then moved on through Didcot and Stevenage to Taunton, ready for demobilisation. To get to Taunton from Hereford we travelled by train under the River Severn, Bristol Channel, a journey of about thirty minutes. At Didcot, I met a man who joined up at the same time as me. He had been working in the Army Offices.

All kit had to be returned except for the greatcoat, the only reminder of my army days apart from my army number, which was clearly imprinted in my head, 97006028. I arrived at Lancaster Castle Station by night train. At last I was going home. There was no transport at that time of night so I started to walk. When I got to Green Aire Station, who should come along in his car but Harry Fawcette, from Ireby Hall. I knew him well because I had often made deliveries to his farm before the war and my spirits lifted. I waved but he sailed by. I was so disappointed. He obviously hadn't recognised me and didn't want to pick up a stranger.

Although rationing took place during the war I think people were healthier for it. Less fats and sugars were eaten because of rationing and we had wholemeal bread instead of white. People became more self sufficient, growing vegetables and a certain amount of fruit. 'Dig for victory', was the slogan at the time. The housewife became more inventive in her cooking using dried eggs and dried milk.

It was a fiddling job for shopkeepers having to mark off and cut out coupons from ration books and sometimes it must have been a worry making their meagre provisions spin out to all their customers.

Mary's mother, Agnes, used to blend their rations of butter and margarine, beating the mixture until it became soft and creamy. This made it go twice as far.

Since there was no imported fruit during the war a great deal of fruit bottling was done. Apples, pears, plums, gooseberries and damsons were preserved in large glass bottling jars. The contents being covered with lightly sugared boiling water and the jars sealed with special tops. Not only did the fruit keep for months, but when opened was absolutely delicious. An occasional batch of oranges would arrive in the country from abroad and then each child would receive an orange. This happened about twice a year. We never saw bananas during the war.

Eggs were put down in large earthenware crocks and covered with isinglass, which was a transparent, almost pure gelatine prepared from the air bladder of certain fish, such as the sturgeon. The eggs kept fresh for weeks.

Rabbits were reasonably easy to come by and Agnes could make a very tasty rabbit pie.

Sweets were rationed and I suppose children missed these greatly, but their teeth benefited.

All children were given cod liver oil and a third of a pint of milk each day, in school. Those who couldn't bear to take the oil were given it in malt. The mixture was quite tasty.

I remember an amusing tale about the black market, it was towards the end of the war a Bentham lad was stopped by the police for not having lights on his bike. When asked his name, the lad replied, "You ought to know. My farm is where you get your black market butter!" I believe the enquiry stopped there.

Fire Service Days

Back of Leyland fire engine - this photo was taken by the River Wenning and the top of old bathing hut is just showing on the right.

Standing left to right - Edmund Wilkinson, Jim Fisher, Noel Bell, (engine) JohnWilcock, Jack Thompson, Jim Guy and Officer from Head Office

Chapter Eight
HOME AGAIN AND THE FIRE SERVICE

My demob in the spring of 1946 saw me back working for Christopher Knowles & Sons, where I remained for about a year.

It was about this time that I joined the Bentham Fire Service. I remained with them from 1946-59. My fireman's number was 1683. Bert Slinger was the officer-in-charge. Jim Guy, John Wilcock, Jimmy Robinson, Jack Bell's son, Noel and Edmund Wilkinson were all members. Our West Riding Station covered the immediate area but if there was a really serious fire, Bentham, Settle and Hornby Stations joined forces.

We were provided with uniforms. The service was voluntary, however if we were called out at night then we were paid five shillings at first and later ten shillings a night. We wore leather boots with long calf length tops. Payment for night duty was made monthly and part was kept out towards the Fireman's Benevolent Fund, the money being used in case of accidents or other misfortunes. A warning siren called the fire-fighters to the station and alarm bells were installed in each of their houses.

Only once did we have two barn fires in one day and the strange thing was, that both barns belonged to farmers called Faraday, one from Sunderland House, above Burton-in-Lonsdale and the other from Low Bentham, in the house near the railway bridge. Both Faradays were related, the uncle at Low Bentham and his nephew at Sunderland House.

We were once called out to a fire at Wennington and when we arrived, the owner, being a semi-invalid was still in bed. He was brought outside and we returned to the house to find the seat of the fire. It seemed to be billowing from behind the skirting boards. When we prised them off, we found smouldering newspapers stuffed into every crevice. The owner said it was to stop the draught!

One night fire broke out at Ribblehead at a farm belonging to a Mr Dowbiggin. I was driving and the lane to the farm was so narrow that we couldn't get the engine through, so we had to use a hand pump with a small engine, which was driven by the distant large engine. In the earlier days our engine carried about two hundred gallons of water and depended mainly on available water hydrants for its supply. Our later engine carried six hundred gallons in case there were no nearby mains.

Hydrants were tested each month when six of our twelve firemen went out with the engine. River water was used whenever possible. This sometimes involved using hundreds of yards of hose with small pumping engines at intervals. This system was used when we pumping water up from the River Greta at Burton-in-Lonsdale, to its church on the hill. After each exercise, the hoses were taken to Angus's Fire Armour Factory, in Bentham, where they were tested for leaks and hung up to dry in the tower there before being rolled and packed away on the engine. I was never afraid of heights and frequently climbed the tower to hang the hoses. The way to the top was by wall ladder and the only things between me and the floor about a hundred feet below, were half a dozen joists, over which the long lengths of hose were draped. The engine was then returned to Crossley's Garage, on Bentham's Main Street, where it was cleaned and polished. Our suits, boots and helmets were kept in a room above the garage which was reached by a narrow staircase. This room was also used as the Fire Station Office and Tom Bibby, who worked for Pye's the Corn Merchant next to the Railway Station kept the books for us. He was a good clerk.

We attended many barn fires, some small and some enormous needing several Fire Services and several days to extinguish the flames. I remember one such fire about a mile from Airton. We were all struggling to remove the burning and smouldering hay from the barn. A nearby smaller barn, not alight, housed quite a large family of owls which hindered us by constantly bombarding us from all angles. It was really quite dangerous. I suppose they were protecting their young. A farmer could not claim on his insurance unless the hay had been under cover for six weeks.

One evening we were called out to a fire at Robert Hall, above Low Bentham. It was a barn fire next to buildings with livestock. We got the cows out into the yard and then discovered a terrified raging bull in the barn next door. Bert Slinger was in charge and after weighing up the situation he sent us in to bring it out. We were as scared as the bull! We needed to cut the rope which tethered it. It was making such a racket that we hardly dared look inside. Fortunately there was a wooden partition between us and the bull, so we were able to lean over with difficulty and cut through the restraining rope. Once released, the bull rushed out into the yard and quietened considerably when it mingled with the cows!

Once when I was still working at C Knowles & Sons, I arrived at work about six o'clock one morning to find the paraffin house alight. Bob Foster had been in earlier to fill the oil lamps for Dinah's flat cart and he thought that a stray spark may have escaped from his pipe. When I opened the door I couldn't get near for the heat. Our diligent Fire Service soon had the fire under control and luckily there wasn't a great deal of damage.

Another fire happened in Leslie Reid's shop, in Main Street, Bentham. It was a wooden hut across from Brown & Whittaker's. It was really a cycle shop but Leslie also sold boots and shoes and did repairs. When the weather was fine, Leslie's father spent most of his days sitting at the door of the shop smoking his pipe. Leslie enjoyed singing and had a wonderful falsetto voice. He was a member of Bentham Operatic Society and could often be heard warbling away at the back of his shop. The fire started suddenly and the hut was there one minute and a short time later, was just a pile of smouldering ashes. Thankfully nobody was hurt. It was never rebuilt and Leslie's poor father missed all his friendly chats with passers by.

Watershed Mill, near Settle, once had a very bad fire. Several local Fire Services attended and engines with turntables were brought from Wakefield. As usual, I was sent up on to the roof. It was a three storey building. All went well until the water was turned on below. The force of the water caught me off balance. It was by sheer good fortune that I wasn't swept off the roof. It took several days to extinguish the blaze. The Wakefield Team brought their own canteen so that they could have food prepared and stay on the job. Bentham firefighters came home in the evening so they could be fit for work the next day. We never lost pay for attending fires.

One winter's night, when the snow lay thick, we were called out to a derailment at Settle. An axle came off an approaching goods train which ran into a passenger train coming down from the north, forcing it off the rails into a siding by the bridge. Debris lay all around in the snow and sadly four people lost their lives. Because of the steep gradient approaching Settle, I understand that engine breaks have to be applied twenty miles back in order to be able to pull up at Settle. Another time railway wagons were alight at Eldroth. Apparently their braking system had seized causing over heating. It wasn't a very serious fire and we soon had it under control.

Once when the Queen's train spent the night in a specially built siding at Clapham Station, we were called into service to fire watch all through the night. The Duke of Edinburgh and his attendants crossed the station yard to the Flying Horeshoe Inn but for some unknown reason didn't stay for the meal that had been prepared for them. The station master at that time was Peter Coulton and early the next morning he lined all the school children along the platform, so that they could wave to the Queen as the train pulled out of the station.

We very seldom begrudged being called out to a fire but I do remember the grumbles when we were called out to Greta Bank, at Burton-in-Lonsdale, to a shed fire. You see, Bentham were playing Lancaster in a football final and we all wanted to support our team.

Fire fighting wasn't our only job. We sometimes had to pump out floodwater. There was a girls' finishing school down by the River Wenning, in Bentham. It was called, 'Hillcroft'. When there had been excessive rain the cellar used to flood and had to be pumped out. Potatoes, which were always stored down there, had to be kept on high shelves to protect them from the water.

A call from Ingleton one evening sent us hurrying off to the Masons Arms Hotel. The cellar was flooding. When we investigated the water was so deep that the floating barrels were bumping against the ceiling. It was an all night job.

I was with the Fire Service for thirteen years and found the work very rewarding. When I left I was presented with a clock and a commemorative shield.

Wednesday Market Days in the 1950's in High Bentham - still as popular! Above is the Main Street and below a fruit stall on School Hill   *John Houghton*

Chapter Nine

'WESTLEIGH' AND THE TRAVELLING LIBRARY

In 1954, Mary, Agnes and myself, moved from Grassrigg to Westleigh, in Goodenber Road, Bentham. After the death of Christopher Knowles, his estate was left to his widow, Agnes. After her day, all proceeds of the will had to be shared equally between their three children, George, Mary (my wife) and Margaret. George and Margaret wanted their money out early, so we sold Grassrigg for eleven hundred pounds to pay them their dues. Mary's share and what little money Agnes had left bought Westleigh. Mary's mother continued to live with us until her death, on 24th November 1960.

Our son, John, was in the army out in Austria at the time of the move and when he came home on leave, completely forgot about the change of address and went sailing up to Grassrigg. He got quite a shock when the new occupants opened the door.

He was demobbed early in 1955 and whilst playing a tennis match at Cowan Bridge met his future wife June Tiler, a girl from Burton-in-Lonsdale. She was teaching in Leeds at the time and every Friday evening, he would hurry down to meet the train bringing her home for the weekend. Then away they would go to Burton on the combination motorcycle, a smart Golden Flash with a Watsonian sidecar.

An amusing incident occurred whilst they were courting. June's mother had a large fluffy ginger cat, who was called 'Marmalade'. He took a great fancy to John's sidecar and unbeknown to John, would travel back to Bentham with him, only to appear as he rode down Robin Lane, into Bentham. It was most embarrassing to be seen riding with a ginger tom gazing through the sidecar window. John made many journeys back to Burton with that cat. One night, it was late when he arrived home plus the cat and Mary suggested, that he leave it in the garage until morning. She gave the cat milk and he slept in his favourite place, in the sidecar.

June and John saw Marmalade approaching the sidecar one day and watched to see how he managed to get in there. They were amazed to see him skilfully undo the studs on the sidecar apron and hide down inside. No amount of tapping on the side or calling brought him out but after that John knew his secret and Marmalade's motorcycling days were over!

June and John were engaged in the spring of 1956 and married on 13th October of the same year. They have three children, Mark, Jayne and Simon, who have all obtained university degrees and are doing well.

Mary's elder brother George had a good friend called James Butterfield who had gone to Canada to live and work. He sent George such glowing letters about the country, that at the age of about thirty he decided to follow his pal out there. He left behind him his fiancée, Margaret Batty with the promise to send for her if the conditions were good. She was duly sent for and they were married immediately. It was a double wedding. James Butterfield and his girlfriend were married at the same time. The fourth year was so severe with frost, ice and rain that they lost all their crops and of course their income, so had to come back to England. Mary's mother Agnes sent money for their fares home. George always called his mother, 'Agnes' never mother. I borrowed a new Ford Ten, from Bert Hemmings to meet them at Liverpool and took Edwin Jackson with me for company. He had always been friendly with George and was keen to meet him again.

The Ford was anything but satisfactory. It was difficult to steer through traffic because it constantly pulled to the left. They were waiting for us with their young son, John, who was just over a year old and we brought them safely home. They went to live at Westhouse, near Ingleton, and started a coal business there. The business did very well and George sold it when he retired.

During the war Mary, was the Bentham Librarian. The library was held once a week in the Town Hall, for one hour every Wednesday evening. Since there was no proper Library building, the books had to be stored in flatish wooden boxes and locked away after each library session for safe keeping. Mr Sanderson used to unpack the boxes for Mary and display the books on long tables. He also packed up afterwards.

After the war, whilst I was still with Christopher Knowles & Sons, I took over Mary's library job and after about a year, I saw a job advertised in the Yorkshire Post. It was for a 'Travelling Library Assistant'. This seemed rather mysterious because there were no travelling libraries at that time (early 1947) but nevertheless, I applied for it. Travelling libraries were the brainchild of West Riding Council's, Wakefield Headquarters. The man in charge of the scheme was a retired army officer and he and his secretary came over to Bentham to interview the applicants. I got the job, which was to do a survey of the North West Riding to find out if a travelling library would be of use in the area. The pay wasn't too exciting but at least it was more than I received from Christopher Knowles & Sons.

A light French Citroen vehicle was provided to go round outlying farms and villages, which included Gargrave, Long Preston, Hellifield, Settle, Clapham, Ingleton, Burton-in-Lonsdale, Bentham, Low Bentham, Ireby, Slaidburn, Bell Busk, Newby, Sedbergh and many of their schools. I also went to Malham Tarn and Wigglesworth. The Citroen had a gravity feed fuel system and steep hills had to be approached backwards.

Residents of villages with libraries were rather resentful at first but when they realised that we were only allowed to stop at least one mile from any village, they no longer objected. So from then on it was full steam ahead. A timetable was drawn up with each place timed according to its size. Five minutes was allowed for an individual farm. Exceptions were made for invalids or the disabled, when we were then allowed to stop outside their houses, even within a village.

The next thing on the agenda was to obtain a suitable vehicle for the job. An ex-war department, Bedford chassis with a six cylinder engine, was purchased by the department and sent to Halifax, to have a body built that could be fitted out with shelves to carry books. I went to Halifax to collect it. I was surprised to find

Crossleys Garage, Low Bentham Road, Bentham, in 1940's

103

how hilly the area was and how very black all the buildings were. I drove that particular vehicle for thirteen years and when it had to be exchanged I received a letter from Wakefield, saying that it was the best kept van in the fleet, which had now extended to twenty. Of course, I washed it down every week and polished and cleaned it out thoroughly.

When the travelling library eventually got off the ground, household rates went up one penny per week. At first people complained but later realised the advantages of this excellent service.

My next larger van was a diesel, which was one of the first diesels on the road at the time. I had problems with it at first because either water or condensation got into the fuel system but Arthur Tustin, who worked at Crossley's Garage, soon got it sorted. Occasionally I found a shelter for my vans otherwise they had to stand outside. The second van in particular was bad to start on winter mornings but seldom let me down when once I got it started.

All books from North West Libraries were exchanged either at Earby, Otley or Wakefield. Earby, was the regional area depot and the books were housed in an ex-music hall, in Water Street. Mr Richardson was in charge of this department. I remember the many stairs on the metal circular staircase which had to be climbed before reaching the book store at the very top.

Once when struggling up the stairs with heavy boxes of books I slipped a disc. I tried my own remedies and visited several doctors without success. Finally I went to visit a Mr Hodkinson, a bone specialist in Nelson. I managed to get a lift in a milk lorry which happened to be travelling to Barnoldswick collecting churns on the way, then on by bus to Nelson.

Mr Hodkinson had many patients who sat on long benches around the large room. He started his surgery at six in the morning in order to cater for the mill workers. When it was time for the next patient to go in a red light came on in the corner. When it was my turn to see him he quickly tapped the disc back in with a small hammer, my back was sore at first but quickly improved. The treatment cost five shillings. About a couple of years later, I had a recurrence of back trouble and visited him at his rooms at Preston. This time I travelled by train to Preston, then by taxi to Mr Hodkinson's rooms. It was the same procedure as before but this time before I came out, he gave me five large bottles of medicine, which to me looked like clear water, with instructions to take some everyday. He said my back would be better within the month and it was. Apart from occasional bouts of lumbago, my back since then has been reasonably strong. The charge was again five shillings and I found it rather embarrassing, travelling back on the bus with these five large bottles, clinking in my carrier bag!

On odd occasions I got lost whilst driving the library van. Once when travelling to Leeds, via Bradford, I got lost in the foggy darkness. I drove on until I saw what I knew to be a sign post. I got out of the van with my torch and scaled the post to read the directions at the top. I did this on more than one occasion. Signs were not illuminated in those days.

The very first time I took the van out to test the route it got dark very early and

Out and about in the Dales with the Library van in the 1960's at Pen-y-ghent, Stainforth.

Margaret Lofthouse and Jim with a friendly collie (photographer's dog)

there was thick snow. The first place I called at was Clapham. Then I took a roundabout route and came back by the Green Smithy above Bentham. The snow was so thick by this time that progress was slow. My heavy-duty tyres saved the day and a whole queue of vehicles followed me safely into Bentham. There was a terrific snowfall that year but not as great as in the winters of 1939 and 1940, when all traffic came to a standstill. Buses and cars were buried, sheep had to be sought out and rescued and it took us almost three days to dig out the snow from Kings Street.

I was once travelling to Wakefield, via Bradford and Leeds, on a book exchange visit when one of the rods from the accelerator snapped and I drew to a halt outside a mill. I called to ask where I could get help. The man in charge of the mill was on holiday but he was kindness itself. He quickly soldered the broken rod and I was able to continue my journey. I must say that I met many such kind people on my travels.

In the early days of the travelling library we advertised our presence by taking the van onto the showfield at various country shows, such as Bentham, Airton, Hellifield and once to Long Preston, on Racing Day. It was surprising the number of people who became interested in our service.

One of the places I really enjoyed visiting was Malham Tarn. We reached it through a cutting in the rock face. Occasionally pieces fell down and had to be removed before we could get through. The house itself was a study centre run by a man and his wife. They were so friendly that we often stayed to have lunch there. At that time we were given a two shilling dinner allowance but that was soon discontinued and we took flasks and sandwiches. The view of the tarn as we came through the cutting was magnificent with gleaming water and hosts of water birds to greet us.

The man in charge of the study centre frequently travelled around the country lecturing on flora and fauna. On a fateful evening, he was travelling back from one such lecture when he was involved in a car accident and was killed. There is a bust of him carved in the rock at the tarn and it is a very good likeness.

Once when delivering books there, there was a very heavy fall of snow and we couldn't get the van out. We had to get home as best we could but we were younger then and long treks didn't bother us. Believe it or not, the snow became so thick that the van was left there for a month. When eventually it could be moved, it amazingly started first time!

All my librarians had spent three years training and were sent to me to 'finish them off'! Although, most were extremely pleasant and helpful, some of them nearly finished me off! My first librarian was a man who stayed with me for about a year.

My second was Miss Margaret Lofthouse. She was a very lively girl who came from Bradford. Most of her surplus energy was taken up in rock climbing. Her climbing skills were taught to her by Chris Bonnington and I'm sure he would find her to be an excellent pupil. She was related to the two Lofthouse sisters who wrote and illustrated books about Yorkshire. Mary invited her to tea occasionally and each time Margaret insisted on doing some gardening for us. There was no

Mary Butterfield

What the snow was like and how the drifts were. This was taken in Robin Lane, High Bentham on 31st January 1940.

need as I always tried to keep our garden immaculate but it seemed to please her to help out. She never stopped dashing about and once when she was running down Station Road to catch her train home, her suitcase flew open spilling its contents all over the road! She caught her train after scooping everything hurriedly into her case and running like the wind!

She certainly knew her job and did it extremely well. I was sorry when she left to go to work in Canada where she now has a very good job in the Library Service. She married over there and I think she has two or three children. Several other librarians followed in Margaret's footsteps, including a university lady in her fifties who stayed for six months, an Irish girl who stayed for twelve months and a young girl who was rather lame, who stayed for about a year. Mr Lawson from Burton-in-Lonsdale was the longest serving librarian and stayed with me about three years. He was a quiet, charming man, who between his work on the library van, looked after his invalid wife.

Besides full time librarians, there were several temps. One was a man from Wakefield. I used to pick him up at Giggleswick Station and drop him back there at night. He worked shifts with Miss Peggy Proctor. My last temp was a girl called Miss Lund from Hellifield.

Once whilst travelling home from Dent with one of my female assistants we got stuck in very heavy snow. I took some top stones from the walls to put under the wheels but replaced them once we got mobile.

In a farm up at Wharfe, near Austwick, lived a man who was very keen on horse breeding. He bred hunters and race horses and made gaps through most of his walls to provide a proper race course for them to ensure they had plenty of exercise. One day he called at the travelling library to see if we had any books on horse breeding. We traced the most suitable books for his needs to America and he was greatly surprised when they arrived in a very short time. A six months period was the general time allowed from ordering to the return of these books.

During all my time with the Library Service I had only two minor accidents. Once when I was driving back from Clapham, I had just passed Butts Farm, when I drew level with a stretch of wall which extended out into the road. A sheep suddenly darted out from behind the wall, ran straight into my van and was killed instantly. I had to make three reports, one for Wakefield, one for the Regional Office, plus diagrams etc and one for me to keep. The second accident happened at Hellifield whilst we were parked having a lunch break. A car came down the slight hill, skidding on the snow and ice, lost control and ran into my van. Thankfully there was not too much damage.

Sometimes we came across emergencies, such as the time we came saw Tommy Clark, collapsed in the snow above the Green Smithy. He had climbed out from his van in which he made deliveries of meat, eggs and other dairy products and had a heart attack. Fortunately, he had another man with him and help was already on its way.

I remained with the Library Service for twenty-three years until my retirement at the age of sixty-six. I should have retired twelve months earlier but Head Office asked me to stay on for another year. Since I enjoyed the job I was delighted to do so.

I must say, that after my retirement from the Library Service, I missed all the wonderful people that over the years I had grown to know so well. Their chatter, their news and anecdotes made our days enjoyable and interesting and I can still remember the names of most of the farms and outlying places where we called and the skill required to drive the van into the more inaccessible places. It's great to look back on those happy days!

Mary and Jim just after Jim retired from the Library in 1960's

Friends Meeting House, High Bentham, taken in July 1999. This is where Mary and Jim were caretakers for many years.

Anne Bonney

Chapter Ten

RETIREMENT

I always enjoyed my garden, both at Grassrigg and Westleigh and found great pleasure in growing flowers and vegetables. In the house garden at Westleigh I grew mostly roses at the front and the back. I kept a neat little lawn and the drive had a long privet hedge down the side which I always cut with shears.

There was space for allotments at the Town End behind the Horse and Farrier and I rented a large plot. I grew all our vegetables and any surplus, Mary sold. I always grew far more than we needed and people appreciated freshly picked vegetables.

When the Cementation Company water pipes were installed in the 1960's, they ran close to Low Bentham and many of Angus's workers quit their jobs to work on the pipeline which supplied water from Thirlmere and Stocks Reservoir. As soon as the pipeline was completed in the area the workers who had left Angus's were fortunate to be given back their jobs.

After retirement I went to look after Tom Jackson's garden for him. He lived in Main Street and worked at the Conservative Club in Bentham in the evenings. Although he wasn't a well man he worked three days a week at Barclays Bank, in Ingleton. When he became too infirm to work he recommended me for his Bank job, which consisted of counting the silver, copper and notes and checking the balance before closing time. Every evening the money was transferred to Bentham Bank leaving a small overnight reserve.

As soon as the Bank was opened in the morning it was my job to search the premises and make sure that everything was in order. If there was a cash shortage during the day, I was sent to the National Westminster Bank across the road to collect money. Old banknotes were brought in from time to time and smelled strongly of manure. When the Government changed the style of the notes, some of the farming community from the outlying places, brought in bundles of notes to be exchanged. Frequently, the smell on the notes was so strong, that we had to take them to Settle Paper Mill to be incinerated! I stayed at the Bank for three years working three days a week and thoroughly enjoyed it. I was always given a lift into Ingleton by one or another of the tellers (cashiers) and one had a Jaguar motor car. That was always a smooth ride.

During the years I worked in the Bank, I spent the other three days gardening at different places. I went to Hornby Castle twice a week. It was owned by Mr Battersby. He was a great employer and always appreciated the work I did. He often came to chat whilst I worked and would occasionally turn his hand to a bit of gardening. The terraces had three beautiful magnolia trees which flowered gloriously in the spring when the lawns were surrounded by hosts of daffodils and narcissi. There was a walled garden with Espaliers (fruit trees or ornamental shrubs trained to grow in a flat plane against the walls) and also a large vegetable plot to keep in order and shrubs and trees to be trimmed. The top lawn had quite a big round cemented pool with a fountain, water lilies and lots of frogs. I stopped working there when Mr Battersby died quite suddenly.

After leaving the castle, I worked at Bentham Grammar School three days a week. The driveway at the left handside had trees and shrubs, that were really overgrown and it was my job to sort them out. Also the border and lawns to the approach needed attention. I gardened at other Grammar School properties, ie Ford House and Collingwood House, which had been the first Grammar School for boys in Bentham. Mary's brother, George attended there as a boy. It was owned by the Parish Council and the first headmaster was a First World War military man who had won the Victoria Cross. He was very well thought of in Bentham and the fact that he was always seen to be smoking Woodbines earned him the nickname, 'Woodbine Willie'! If it rained on gardening days I cleaned the boys' showers or assisted Mr Wheelden, the plumber. His father, Frank, used to play football for Bentham and was known as, 'The Tank', because when once he was in possession of the ball, there was no stopping him. He would bulldoze his way through to the goal.

Bentham had a good football team in those days and John and myself liked to follow their matches. I remember the five Chapel boys who used to play at different times. Their names were George, Jimmy, Tommy, Eric and Francis. They were all very athletic and excellent footballers. The team won the Lancashire Junior Shield about this time. Billy Noble, another player played in goal until he was sixty!

Once I travelled pillion on John's motorbike to Hellifield, to watch the team play. I was reprimanded by John for constantly leaning the wrong way on corners making steering hazardous. Billy Noble was in goal as usual and two minutes before time he was facing a penalty. He dived the wrong way but by a stroke of luck his retreating foot caught the ball and saved the day! Bentham won by one goal!

On Saturday mornings I sometimes went to help John in his joinery workshop in Hornby. I primed new windows and doors and bagged up sawdust and wood chippings.

Around 1958, Mary's mother Agnes became infirm and needed a lot of looking after. She was incontinent and Mary developed dermatitis on her arms from all the washing. We didn't have a washing machine at that time. She also got an arthritic knee from trailing up and downstairs. Margaret offered to have Agnes for a while much to our relief but after one week, she said that she and Edgar were exhausted and Agnes came back. After eighteen months Dr Elizabeth insisted that Agnes should go into Harden Bridge Hospital, near Austwick, to give Mary a rest. This meant visiting two or three times a week, which Mary and Margaret did diligently. It meant long bus journeys but at least when Mary got home, she could rest. Whilst at Harden Bridge Hospital, Agnes fell and broke her hip. She developed pneumonia and died on 24th November, 1960.

Mary had never been allowed to cook or bake. Agnes had always done that side of things. She was well known for her Christmas and wedding cakes and travellers to the shop and tradesmen to the house always reserved visiting, for Agnes's baking days, when they were treated to freshly baked scones and other delicacies. She also had a wonderful gift with herbs, poultices and ointments and the local doctor would send patients suffering from boils or sceptic wounds, to Agnes for treatment. They had great faith in her and showed their appreciation by bringing her farm butter, eggs, bacon or cheese.

Mary soon enjoyed her new task and was a brilliant cook. She made delicious meals for us and often made soups, cakes and dainty snacks for neighbours, especially if they were off colour.

Between the years of 1953-73, Mary and I were caretakers at the Friends Meeting House in Main Street, Bentham. It had been used for Meeting since 1864. We cleaned, kept the keys and turned the heating on and off for Meetings, jumble sales and other family occasions. The doors were usually left open, until late one night the collection box was broken into. Then we had to keep it locked at all times.

Many churches were being robbed and some even ransacked, so had to be kept locked. It seems so sad to have to lock the doors of our places of worship. If you want to look round, or sit quietly in a church which hasn't a full time warden or caretaker, you have to seek out the keeper of the keys.

We were caretakers for twenty years in all. I used to clean the gutters and tend the gardens. All this was voluntary work and after nineteen years, we felt we needed a rest but the Committee offered us one shilling a week to continue a bit longer. We agreed and after six months we were paid two shillings a week. After another six months the building was sold in 1973 and the Meeting went back to Calf Cop. Philip Harvey was one of the elders at Meeting and his daughter, Sheila, borrowed one of his vehicles and helped me move everything back to Calf Cop. We had a good Meeting at that time with at least forty to fifty members. Sadly our numbers have declined as our older Friends die and younger ones move away.

We had monthly Meetings at Preston Patrick, Settle, Brigflatts, near Sedbergh, Skipton and Bentham. Annual open air meetings were held at Firbank Fell, when we gathered round the rock from which George Fox had preached. We also had twice a year Meetings at Airton.

Monthly Meetings were always enjoyable. Different people made refreshments for these occasions, usually in the earlier years, Mary and Margaret, when the Meeting was held at Bentham.

The four of us, Mary, Margaret, Edgar and myself always helped with others when sales of works and other Quaker events took place. Sadly, Edgar had a stroke in 1969. Although he recovered physically, his mental state was much impaired. He died in 1971.

My dear sister Agnes, died in Australia aged 84 years on 6th August, 1986. After Edgar's death, Margaret had continued to live at 'Ash Lea' in Robin Lane, where she stayed until July 1992, when she came to live at Abbeyfield House, in Bentham. She was very happy there and died peacefully on 17th November, 1996.

In the early seventies, I bought a little car from John. It was a red Fiat 600. This broadened our horizons tremendously. We had many trips out nearly always taking Margaret with us. The car made us more independent and we went off for holidays to Scotland and the East Coast. Latterly we stayed in Morecambe at the West End in a lovely flat, over a chemists shop and then in a flat on Sandylands. We always enjoyed these short breaks. Margaret came with us as there was always a spare bedroom.

Around 1980, we went on holiday to the Isle of Man, with June, John and family. It's a beautiful island and John hired a mini-bus for the seven of us and managed to show us most of the island. We had a wonderful holiday.

We used to visit friends who lived in Abbeyfield Homes in Morecambe and also visited the Cove, in Silverdale.

I drove until I was eighty-eight years old, when I had my first little bump as I was backing out of my driveway. The accelerator stuck down at floor level and I couldn't get my toe under to pull it up. The car shot backwards out of the drive and across the road into a low wall which was partly demolished. Fortunately the street was empty at the time and my grandson and I were unhurt. After that I decided to call it a day as far as driving was concerned.

Mary developed bronchial asthma in her early eighties and gradually grew worse each winter. Regular hospital visits began as her breathing became more laboured. I was not too happy driving into Lancaster because the traffic system was always changing and this worried me, so June always accompanied Mary on these visits. Chest infections followed, each one worse than the last. One morning I rang June to say that Mary was very ill. June quickly got the doctor and he sent for the ambulance. When June returned from the hospital she said that John would take us in the next day. The phone rang early next morning asking us to go down immediately. We were there within the hour but were just too late. On 11th March, 1993, Mary had taken and enjoyed her last cup of tea. She fell asleep and died peacefully. She was interred in the peaceful little churchyard at Calf Cop.

I was devastated and could not imagine life without Mary. She had been my mainstay. After Mary's death, June came over to Bentham every day. I realised that she could not do this for ever, so I applied for a room at Abbeyfield House, in Bentham, where I came to live in July 1993.

I try to keep myself as mobile as possible. In my early days at Abbeyfield House, I used to walk to Low Bentham and back every day, a distance of about three miles. I remember one particular day after walking down into Low Bentham and standing on the bridge looking over into the river, I saw Bert Cornthwaite in a nearby paddock. He was mustering his sheep and trying without success to get them into a trailer. After watching several unsuccessful attempts, I called over and suggested that if he lifted a sheep and carried it into the trailer the others would follow. He was pleased to find that my suggestion worked and quickly secured the tailboard, with his flock safely inside.

On Christmas Eve morning 1995, I walked into Low Bentham as usual and slipped on some ice which had formed from water running out of a gateway. I fell and broke my left femur and was in hospital for six weeks. Thankfully, after having a plate in my leg I recovered quite well, although of course I can't walk as far. I still try to have two or three short walks a day but tend to get rather stiff at times and suffer from the usual aches and pains associated with old age. I stopped attending Meeting after this, although good friends offered me lifts on Sundays, I found the effort of getting my legs into a car was too much for me and the long sit was painful.

June visits me every Wednesday, when we reminisce about my early life and have an enjoyable day together. John and June visit me every Sunday afternoon bringing with them any of my grandchildren who might be at home.

We started recording from my earliest memories (aged two) to the present day and sought out relevant photographs. It has taken us eleven months to complete. Originally it was done solely for my family and friends. I have now shared it with you and hope you have enjoyed it and gain as much pleasure from the reading as we have had from the writing: the story of my life as I remember it!

June (author of this book) together with Jim on an afternoon early in 1999 at Abbeyfield House, Bentham   *Anne Bonney*

Helm Press have also published

'A Westmorland Shepherd', his life, poems and
songs by Fred Nevinson

'Elephants on the Line' Tales of a Cumbrian Railwayman
(1947 - 1995) by John Cottam

'Dear Mr Salvin' The story of the building
of a 19th century Ulverston church -
edited by John Marsh and transcribed by Anne Bonney

For further details telephone (015395) 61321
or write to Helm Press, 10 Abbey Gardens, Natland,
Kendal, Cumbria LA9 7SP